W9-CKF-460

GOOD HOME COOKING

BREADS & BISCUITS

By Linda Campbell Franklin
Designed by Sara Bowman

An Aromatic Collection of Over 75 Recipes
Selected from Good Home Cooks
All Over the United States and from Antique
Receipt Books, Together with Original Recipes,
&
Generous Room to Write in 35 Recipes of Your Own.

Tree Communications, Inc.
New York City

© 1981, Tree Communications, Inc. All rights reserved. No part of this work may be reproduced or transmitted in any form by any means, electronic or mechanical, including photocopying and recording, or by any information storage or retrieval system without permission in writing from the publisher.

Published in the United States by
Tree Communications, Inc.,
250 Park Avenue South,
New York City, New York 10003.
Printed in the United States of America.

ISBN 0-934504-08-3

Library of Congress Catalog Card No. 81-51420

This book was typeset in Goudy Old Style by David E. Seham Associates, Inc. Color separations were made by National Colorgraphics, Inc. The paper is 70 lb. Warren Olde Style, cream, supplied by Baldwin Paper Company. The book was printed and bound by R. R. Donnelley & Sons Company.

I have received some very upper crust help on this book of recipes! I congratulate the designer, Sara Bowman, on her fine eye. She and I are particularly grateful for the imagination and good taste of Lorna Bieber, assistant designer for the book. We also want to thank Susan Hunt Yule for her drawings of fancy rolls on page 85.
I would never have found the wonderful poem on Hush Puppies that appears on page 52 were it not for a cookbook —now in its ninth printing —called Favorite Recipes of The Lower Cape Fear, *published by the Ministering Circle of Wilmington, N.C. Copies are available from Mrs. Alan Marshall, 2006 Randolph Road, Wilmington 28403. My thanks also to Ruth Forst Michel for her thoughtful research. I wish to salute ephemerists everywhere —the excellent scrap-pickers who collect Victorian trade cards and postcards such as those decorating the pages of this book. Pictures on pages 8 and 9 from* 300 Years of Kitchen Collectibles *by L. C. Franklin, Books Americana, 1981. Finally, without the rallying 'round of all the following good home cooks, we'd have no book at all: Cheryl Roberts, Louise Bruner Orr, Nancy VandenBerg, Jimmie Peattie, A. C. Lind, Martha Rayburn, Lois Douglass, Rose Mary Fischer, Mrs. E. C. Hobbitt, Dot and Jack Roberts, the late Helen Tryon, Mary Mac Franklin, Beatrice Huckaby, Kate Wyckoff, Grace McFarland, June Folsom, Mario Montrose, Hannah K. Wright, Barbara Tomkinson Reich, Craig Tomkinson, Robert D. Franklin, John McBurney, Willie Lee Burton, Margaret Faulconer Minich, Rachel Cohen, David Nolty, Esther Jean Lee, Mary Liz Johnson, The Raymond Parkers, the late Maggie Davis, Mrs. Haskell S. Rhett and Beulah Walters. De gustibus!*

Write us about other books in the Keepbook™ series.

This Book Belongs to

Lorrie 9/82

Linda C. Franklin, Editor

Sara Bowman, Designer

OLD FASHIONED KEEPBOOKS

Rodney Friedman, Bruce Michel & Ron Gross, Proprietors

TREE COMMUNICATIONS, INC.

250 Park Avenue South

New York, New York 10003

"Keep us in your memories."

Dear Friends,

Bread recipes used to scare me to death, but no more. I hope that any of you who are shy about sticking your hands down into a mass of dough will gain courage from this book of shared recipes.

The bread, biscuit, roll, muffin and cracker recipes here offer a variety of American flavors. Many are based on corn, pumpkin and squash-- foods the Indians showed the first settlers how to prepare. The recipes using peanuts and yams are examples of the long-lasting contribution of the Africans brought here as slaves. Other recipes reflect the diverse ancestry of 20th century Americans. Now we can all make them part of our cooking heritage.

I wish there were some way of starting a lending library of all the thousands of <u>Breads & Biscuits</u> cookbooks which are going to be filled in with treasured family recipes over the next few years! That would truly be in the spirit of the old tradition of recipe-sharing, which probably began with someone asking a friend for, say..."a copye of ye receipt for that tastye lofe of bread."

Happy cooking!

Linda Campbell Franklin

Contents

The following is excerpted from a classic cookbook of the 19th century: The Young Housekeeper's Friend *by Mrs. Cornelius, first published in Boston in 1846. This selection is from the second, 1859, edition. Mrs. Cornelius acknowledges that times have changed. Imagine what she would think of our easy ways —ovens with automatic timers and dials to set the heat!*

∽ Ovens—and How to Heat Them ∾

Stoves and cooking-ranges have so generally taken the place of brick ovens, that the following directions, which were appropriate when this book was first published, will seldom be of use now. Yet, as they may sometimes be needed, they are suffered to remain. It is impossible to give minute directions as to the management of the various kinds of baking apparatus now in use. A few experiments will enable a person of good judgment to succeed with any of them.

A few suggestions in regard to the construction of an oven may be useful. For a family of medium size, an oven holding ten or twelve plates is large enough. There should be two or three bushels of ashes, with dead coals in them, poured over the top, after the first tier of bricks which forms the arch is laid. Then the usual brickwork should be laid over them. The advantage is this,—when the oven is heated, these ashes and coals are heated also, and, being so thick, retain the heat a long time. Five successive bakings have been done in such an oven with one heating; the bread first—then the puddings—afterward pastry—then cake and gingerbread—and lastly custards, which, if made with boiled milk and put into the oven hot, and allowed to stand a considerable time, will bake sufficiently with a very slight heat.

The first time an oven is heated, a large fire should be kept burning in it six or eight hours. Unless this is done it will never bake well.

The size and structure of ovens is so different, that no precise rules for heating them can be given. A lady should attend to this herself, until she perfectly understands what is necessary, and can give minute directions to those she employs. It is easy to find out how many sticks of a given size are necessary for baking articles that require a strong heat; and so for those which are baked with less. To bake brown bread, beans, apples, and other things, all at one time, the oven should be heated with hard wood, and if rather large, so as to be two hours in burning out, it is better. To bake thin cake, and some kinds of puddings, pine wood, split small, answers very well.

After the wood is half burnt, stir the fire equally to all parts of the oven. This is necessary for an equal diffusion of the heat. Do it several times before the oven is cleared. If the oven is to be very full, put in a brick, so that you can have it hot, to set upon it any pan or plate for which there may not be room on the bottom. Be careful that no doors or windows are open near the oven. Let the coals remain until they are no longer red. They should not look dead, but like hot embers. When you take them out, leave in the back part a few to be put near the pans that require most heat, such as beans, Indian pudding, or jars of fruit. Before putting in the things to be baked, throw in a little flour. If it browns instantly, the oven is too hot, and should stand open three or four minutes. If it browns without burning in the course of half a minute, it will be safe to set in the articles immediately. It is often best not to put in those things which require a moderate heat, till those which need a strong heat have been baking ten or fifteen minutes.

A coal scuttle of peat, with less wood, is economical, and gives an equal and very prolonged heat. Many persons use it with pine wood, for their ordinary baking. It takes a longer time to burn out than wood.

It is well to kindle the fire as far back as possible, because all parts of the wood are much sooner on fire than if it is kindled near the mouth of the oven; and if peat is used, it should not be thrown in until the wood is well kindled.

Collecting Antique Bread-Making Utensils

The old days are long gone when outmoded kitchen gadgetry and utensils were hidden in bushel baskets under tables in all but the most country of antique shops and flea market stalls. Collecting all the fascinating tin, wire, enameled iron, cast iron, wood, copper, brass and glass cooks' tools is now very popular. People specialize in different ways: one man accumulated in three years every nutmeg grater he could find, at any price asked, because he wanted to have the best and biggest nutmeg grater collection in the United States. A woman in New York State assembled a complete, working 1930's kitchen in her basement. She has everything from a G.E. monitor-top refrigerator and flowered linoleum floors to decaled cupboards filled with 1930's packages and containers of food. She even wears a period apron when she goes downstairs to cook. Other collectors specialize in a material, such as cast iron or tin; or in a broad functional category—everything relating to cutting and chopping, or everything having to do with making bread.

There are several particularly interesting implements or utensils used in bread-making. Molds are big favorites. This category includes muffin tins with plain or fancy stamped-out cups, fluted tube pans, or cast iron pans for making cornbread corncobs, rolls or popovers. The products of such companies as Wagner Ware, W & L Manufacturing and Waterman are very desirable. Also collectible are blackened tin bread pans—loaf pans in many sizes like those made today, or odd capsule-like hinged pans, singles or doubles, made by Ideal and patented in 1897.

Bread raisers are footed tin or enameled-iron vessels which came in sizes from eight quarts to 21 quarts. They look rather like soup tureens, with high-domed lids and little ear handles. One distinguishing feature is the ventilated lid—small holes near the knob. Bread raisers are hard to find; they are either rusted and dented, often with a handle or knob knocked off, or they are still being used by a second or third generation of devoted bread-makers who cannot foresee the time when they would want to retire their prized possession.

A very special collection can be made of biscuit cutters. Some are simple tin cylinders, about 2″ high with an arched handle. Others have advertising slogans and the brand names of flour, lard or butter stamped on them. A particularly intriguing kind of biscuit cutter is made of aluminum and has a long handle. It is rolled, rather like a lawn mower, over the flattened dough and cuts biscuit after biscuit, perfectly and quickly. Other tinwares include flour sifters and dredgers, graters of every description, measuring cups and spoons. In the late 19th century, Landers, Frary & Clark manufactured a "bread maker"—a sort of pail that was clamped to the table. These came in two-loaf, four-loaf and eight-loaf sizes. None but the most stalwart of bread-makers could hope to turn the crank of the eight-loafer.

If the mellow patina of woodenwares appeals to you, look for rolling pins, mixing spoons and dough boards. Especially nice are round bread boards, with mottoes such as "Give us this day our daily bread" carved around the perimeter. These often doubled as lids for large butter crocks, and some have matching bread knives, the handles of which are also carved.

A whole collection can be made of patented 19th and early 20th century bread knives—with their efficiently designed scalloped or serrated blades. Among the most famous manufacturers or trade names are Tip-Top Boy, Climax, Universal, Aetna, Keen Kutter, Clauss and Christy. I once found a marvelous Tip-Top Boy knife, the painted wooden handle in next-to-new shape, the brass ferrule shining, stuck into a gummy gallon can of paint—it was being used as a paint stirrer. I pulled it out, took it home and it cleaned up perfectly after I soaked the blade in paint remover.

Although not used exclusively for bread making, eggbeaters such as the famous Dover, patented in 1870, are avidly sought by collectors. There are at least 250 different eggbeaters from before 1900. All were scientifically designed to overcome whatever faults the inventor thought other eggbeaters possessed. If one designer claimed that his *beat* the egg, another would rise to the challenge and claim that his *cut* the egg.

At least some of your bread-making tool collection can actually be used. Just remember that before the days of stainless steel (and that means pre-1920) carbon steel was used for knives and tin-plated iron was used for everything from eggbeater blades to pans. Don't scour any old implement with abrasive cleanser, and if you wipe everything dry after washing, you can enjoy almost all the antique gadgets and utensils which look so appealing and often work so well.   LCF

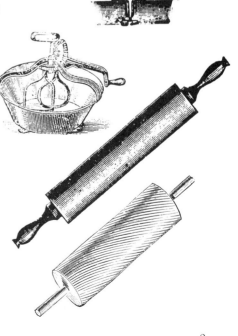

⮞ Bread-Making Pointers ⮜

YEAST. Active dry yeast is easiest to use. Check the expiration date, and always *proof* the yeast by stirring it in warm water. Watch for bubbling "activity." If it is slow, add a pinch of sugar to feed the yeast. Start over with more yeast if nothing happens in five minutes.

FLOUR AND MEAL. All-purpose or bread flours are good for bread-making. High gluten flours, available primarily in health food stores, are good additives. Never use old flour, especially if it smells musty. There's no *best* cornmeal. Choose what you like—stone- or water-ground, yellow or white.

SHORTENING. Baking properties and flavors of vegetable shortening, lard, oil, butter or margarine are all different, but they are pretty much interchangeable. Try to use what is called for, and always use at room temperature.

LIQUIDS. If desired, use dry milk (even low fat) to make milk for recipes. Sour milk can be made by adding a teaspoon of lemon juice. Water or milk must be warmed for many recipes.

SUGAR AND SALT. Both add their own flavor. More important: sugar helps yeast ferment; salt helps control the action of the yeast. Neither, however, is absolutely necessary. Reduce sugar to suit yourself.

KNEADING SURFACE. A "floured surface" can mean a board, countertop or cloth-covered surface. Cloth works beautifully. Use a well-washed, lint free pillowcase, flour sack, piece of sheeting or canvas to make a dough board cover. Sew ties on the corners, or put elastic around edges to make a sort of fitted "bottom sheet" or tape to counter. Dust cloth with flour and knead dough directly on it. The dough won't stick, and neither will you need lots of extra flour.

ALTITUDE. Yeast doughs rise in a shorter time in altitudes over 5,500 feet. Check an almanac or local map for your town's altitude. Also affected is the quantity of yeast needed—halve the amount when you are over 5,500 feet. Watch the dough rise—it may take 15 or 20 minutes less time to rise to double bulk. Quick breads are also affected. If you live over 2,000 feet, reduce each teaspoon of baking powder or baking soda by a quarter teaspoon for every 1,000 feet. For example, at 4,000 feet, reduce 3 teaspoons of baking powder to 2½. You may also need to add a bit more liquid because of greater evaporation. When baking at high altitudes, increase oven temperatures by 15° to 25°—you'll have to experiment.

BAKING PANS. Reduce oven temperature by 25° if you use glass pans. For an equipment list, see page 126.

CRUSTS. Brush dough with cold water before baking for a crusty crust. Brush toward the end of baking with lightly beaten egg whites and water for crisp glazed crust; or with yolk beaten with milk or water for a rich brown glazed crust. Brush with milk a few minutes before bread is done for good color. Brush with butter and cover with a damp cloth, immediately after baking, for a soft tasty crust. Bake with a pan of hot water in the bottom of the oven for a hard crust.

DONENESS. The classic test for yeast breads goes as follows: remove the loaf from the pan and tap the bottom with your forefinger. If it sounds hollow, the bread is done; if there's naught but a dull thud, bake another five minutes and test again. The classic quick bread test is done with a clean broomstraw or wooden toothpick or splinter. Stick it into the center of the loaf and pull it out. A dry stick means done bread.

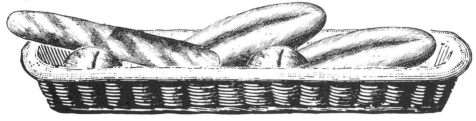

∾ Light Bread ∾

In the South, the name "light bread" refers to leavened white bread—that is, bread raised with yeast or leaven, which is leftover fermented bread dough. This recipe might be called Levitation Bread, from the Latin word levāre which means to raise or lighten. Many variations on this basic recipe are possible: add dried herbs, currents or grated cheese, for example, just before kneading.

Yields: Two loaves

1 envelope dry yeast
1 tablespoon sugar
1 tablespoon salt
½ cup nonfat dry milk
2½ cups warm water
   (105° to 115°F)

3 tablespoons shortening
   or lard
5½ cups all-purpose or bread
   flour
½ cup all-purpose flour
   (reserved)

 Two greased loaf pans approximately 9″ x 5″ x 3″

Mix the yeast, sugar, salt and milk powder in a large mixing bowl and pour in the water. Add the shortening and stir until everything is dissolved. Add three cups of flour and beat vigorously for about two minutes with a wooden spoon. (You may use an electric mixer with dough hooks, medium speed for two minutes.) Next, using the wooden spoon and your fingers, thoroughly mix in as much (2½ to 3 cups) of the remaining flour as needed to make the dough soft but not sticky. In a few minutes you will be able to begin kneading. Turn the dough out onto a floured surface and knead. Push, fold, rotate, push, fold, rotate: keep kneading for eight to 10 minutes, until the dough becomes springy, soft as silk and smooth as satin. Roll ball around in a big lightly-greased bowl to coat the surface. Cover bowl with a dish towel or plastic wrap and place in a warm spot (about 80° to 85°F) for about an hour, or until dough doubles in bulk.

   Punch down to deflate it and knead a few times to express all the yeasty gas. Cut the ball in half, reshape into two flattish ovals and let rest for five minutes. Now fold the edges over, pinch the "seam" to seal it, and place each loaf, seam down, in a greased pan. Cover and put back in warm spot. [*After 20 minutes preheat oven to 400°F.*] The dough ovals will double in bulk in about a half-hour. Prepare tops for crust (see page 10) and place in oven. Bake for 35 to 45 minutes. When done, turn out to cool on racks.

Notes: _____
_____
_____
_____
_____
_____
_____

Date first tried: _____

Notes:_____

_____

_____

_____

_____

_____

_____

_____

Date first tried:_____

∽ Cheryl's Garden Bread ∽

"I was inspired by Bertha Roberts, my grandmother who baked bread and rolls, cakes and pies all the time. Her fresh bread always made my mouth water and I could eat as much as I wanted at her house—as opposed to eating cake or pie that was divided up many ways among the family members. Anyway, one of our delights was to sit at the enamel kitchen table in front of the huge wood stove and eat bread and butter with sugar on it." Recipe by Cheryl Roberts, North Carolina

Yields: Two medium loaves

1 envelope dry yeast	2 cups gluten flour
2 cups warm water (105° to 115°F)	2 cups whole wheat flour
1¼ tablespoons salt	1 cup unbleached white flour (reserved)
1 tablespoon honey	cornmeal
2 cups unbleached white flour	

 One greased baking sheet, sprinkled with cornmeal

In a large mixing bowl, proof the yeast in the warm water. Add the honey and salt. Add the flour one cup at a time, mixing and beating with a wooden spoon. If you need the reserve cup of flour to make a workable dough, add it a bit at a time. Turn dough out on a floured board and knead it for about 10 minutes, to develop the gluten. When the dough is smooth and springy, roll it around in a greased bowl. Cover the bowl with a cloth and let rise in a warm spot (80° to 85°F) until doubled in bulk. This takes about an hour. Punch down and divide into two pieces. [*Here's where you add herbs to one loaf if you wish. See below.*] Shape into two long Italian-style loaves. Arrange on a greased baking sheet, well-sprinkled with cornmeal. Cover with a towel, allow to rest, and rise, for five minutes—out of drafts. [*Meanwhile boil at least a quart of water for the oven.*]

Brush loaves with water, and slash in several places on top with a razor or sharp knife. (See suggestions on page 14.) Place baking sheet in a cold oven with a pan of boiling water on the shelf underneath. *Turn the oven to 400°F and bake 40 to 50 minutes until crusty.* Turn out on a rack to cool.

VARIATION: Stir fry in a tablespoon of butter, a ½ cup each of finely-chopped parsley and chives or scallions, a clove of garlic, minced, and freshly ground pepper. Push dough for one loaf into a rough rectangle. Spread evenly with the herb butter, roll up and seal edges. Let rise 30 to 45 minutes, or until well-rounded. It will not hurt the plain loaf to rise this extra time.

Triticale Whole Wheat Bread

Something new is growing under the sun—without fear of weeds, and undaunted by unfertilized soil. Triticale is a high protein grain, a hybrid combination of rye and wheat. It is widely available in the country's health food stores—those emporiums which are such a boon to today's home bakers. This flour makes a dense loaf that freezes well. Recipe contributed by Louise Bruner Orr, Ohio

Yields: Four small or two medium loaves

1 envelope dry yeast
4 tablespoons honey or brown sugar (or 3 of molasses)
½ cup warm water (105° to 115°)
2 tablespoons melted shortening, or oil
2 teaspoons salt

1½ cup milk, scalded and lukewarm
2 cups triticale flour
1½ cup all-purpose flour
1¾ cups whole wheat flour
¼ cup wheat germ, raw or toasted

 Four greased mini-loaf pans, 5″ x 2½″ x 2¼″, or
Two greased loaf pans 8″ x 4″ x 2½″

In a big mixing bowl, dissolve the yeast and sweetener in water and let stand for five minutes. Now mix in the shortening, salt and milk. Beat in the mixed flours with a wooden spoon, but add only as much as needed to keep the dough from being sticky. Now mix in the wheat germ. When the dough comes away from the sides of the bowl it is ready to knead. Knead for about 10 minutes until springy and smooth. Because of the relatively low amount of white flour, the dough will not feel quite as elastic and satiny as a basic white bread. Roll the dough ball around in a large, lightly-greased bowl and cover with plastic wrap or a tea towel to rise in a warm place (80° to 85°F) for about an hour. (In an electric oven, place the bowl on upper rack and a large pan of boiling water on the lower rack. This keeps the oven warm and moist.)

When doubled in bulk, punch the dough down and allow to rest for five to 10 minutes. Now shape into loaves, place in greased loaf pans, and let rise again, slightly higher than the tops of the pans. This should take about 35 or 40 minutes. [*Preheat oven to 400°F.*] When risen, bake for 15 minutes at 400° and then reduce heat to 350° and bake another 20 to 30 minutes if you make small loaves—longer if you use larger pans. When done, turn out to cool on a rack.

Notes: _____

_____

_____

_____

_____

_____

_____

Date first tried: _____

Notes:_____

_____

_____

_____

_____

_____

_____

Date first tried:_____

Mrs. VandenBerg sometimes uses her scissors to cut cryptic acronyms and messages in the top of the loaves before baking. These cuts let off steam during baking. She also suggests making cinnamon-raisin rolls or balls (see Monkey Bread, page 21) and packing them into a greased Christmas tree cake pan—a "wonderful home-baked present for friends."

∾ Honey Whole Wheat Bread ∾

Part of the fun in this recipe are the cook's directions. We share them with you exactly as she wrote them. Recipe by Nancy VandenBerg, New Jersey

Yields: Four loaves

1 envelope dry yeast	1 cup nonfat dry milk
6 cups warm water (105° to 115°)	8 cups whole wheat flour
1 cup honey	8 cups all-purpose flour
2 tablespoons salt	½ cup bran flakes
4 tablespoons melted butter	½ cup wheat germ

Four greased loaf pans, 8½" x 4½" x 2½"

"Remove rings from fingers and roll up sleeves. Using a very large mixing bowl, stir yeast into water. Add honey, salt, powdered milk and melted shortening. Stir and then add three cups of the white flour. Beat with a whisk until smooth. Add whole wheat flour, remaining white flour, bran flakes and wheat germ gradually, beating with a wooden spoon, until you reach the kneading stage. Turn out on large floured surface. If dough is sticky, sprinkle with white flour as needed. Knead the heck out of it for 10 full minutes, until the dough is elastic. Divide in half and place in two large buttered bowls, turning the dough to coat all over. Cover with a damp tea towel. When double in bulk, punch down with your fist, without removing dough from bowl. Re-cover, and let rise again. When risen, divide in half yet again, making four equal pieces, cover, and let rest for 10 minutes. Pat and/or yank each piece into a rectangular shape (it fights back), about 1" thick. Now roll up jelly-roll fashion and place in greased loaf pans. Slash the tops with a kitchen scissor now or after you've let each loaf rise again until doubled in bulk (about 1" over the top). [*Preheat oven to 375°F.*] Bake for about an hour. All ovens are temperamental, and mine bakes these loaves at 350° in 40 to 45 minutes! When done, remove immediately from the pans and place on a wire rack to cool. Inhale several times. Just about now all the neighbors will come to call, especially if the windows are open. They will look hungry. That's the reason for making four loaves at a clip."

VARIATION: To dress up two of the loaves: combine 1 cup coarsely chopped walnuts, 1 cup raisins, ½ teaspoon each of nutmeg and cinnamon, ½ cup brown sugar, and ¼ cup flour to coat everything. Mash this mixture firmly into the dough rectangle, just before the dough is rolled up "jelly roll fashion." Bake as above.

～ Pumpernickel ～

Pumpernickel is a hearty, moist bread with so much rustic character you expect it to drive up on a tractor! Most people slice it thin and cold, citifying it, but I like warmed chunks of it with lots of butter. The name itself is German, and was first used in 1663, although it was spelled pompernickel. *In Westphalia it meant course rye bread, but in slang it also meant a lout, a coarse fellow.*

Yields: Two to four loaves

2 envelopes dry yeast

¼ cup warm water
   (105° to 115°F)

2½ cups cold water

¾ cup cornmeal

2 tablespoons shortening

2 tablespoons molasses

2 tablespoons baker's
   cocoa (optional)

1 tablespoon salt

1 tablespoon caraway seeds

1½ cups mashed potatoes

3 cups rye flour

2 cups whole wheat flour

1 cup all-purpose flour

½ cup all-purpose flour
   (reserved)

Notes: _____

_____

_____

_____

_____

_____

_____

Date first tried: _____

 Two greased baking sheets, sprinkled with cornmeal

In a small bowl, combine the yeast and warm water. Put the cornmeal in a saucepan and pour the cold water in slowly. Stir *constantly* over medium heat, for about two minutes. When the mixture boils and is thick and smooth, remove from the stove and put into a large bowl. Stir in shortening, molasses, cocoa, salt and caraway seeds. Add the proofed yeast. Blend in the mashed potatoes. Mix the flours together, and gradually add to the cornmeal and yeast, beating until the dough is workable, if somewhat sticky and stiff. Turn out on a surface well-dusted with white flour. Knead for at least 10 minutes, until the dough is smooth and somewhat elastic. Roll the ball around in a greased bowl to coat the surface, cover the bowl and place in a warm spot (80° to 85°F) for about an hour to double in bulk.

Punch down and knead for a few seconds to express gas bubbles. Divide dough in half, thirds or quarters, depending on the size of finished loaves you want (remember the dough will rise again). Rest the dough under a towel for four or five minutes. Form oval or round loaves and place on the greased baking sheet(s) which have been sprinkled with cornmeal. Cover and let rise again for about an hour. [*Preheat oven to 375°F.*] Slash the tops. Bake for 30 to 45 minutes—depending on their size and your oven. When done, turn out on wire racks to cool.

Notes:_____

_____

_____

_____

_____

_____

_____

_____

Date first tried:_____

VARIATION: Form dough into roll-sized equal pieces before the second rising. Form a circle of the slightly-flattened balls, each almost touching its neighbor. Cover and let rise ½ hour on the baking sheet. These rye rings take only about 20 to 35 minutes to bake.

WHEN COMING THRO' THE RYE

⋙ Rye Round Bread ⋘

Maybe it's the power of suggestion, but this rye bread is the best bread for butter-grilled cheese sandwiches I ever tasted. Fry bacon crisp, and build a sandwich with your favorite cheese, bacon and tomato slices, and grill on thin slices of this dense bread. Recipe by Jimmy Peattie, Tennessee

Yields: Two round loaves

3 envelopes dry yeast
1½ cups warm water
  (105° to 115°F)
¼ cup molasses
¼ cup brown sugar
2 teaspoons salt
3 teaspoons caraway seed
1 teaspoon powdered
  summer savory

2 tablespoons melted bacon
  fat (or other shortening)
2¾ cups rye flour
1 cup whole wheat
  (or triticale) flour
2 cups all-purpose flour
1 cup all-purpose
  flour (reserved)

 One large greased baking sheet

In a large mixing bowl, dissolve the yeast in the water and then stir in the molasses, sugar, salt, caraway seeds and savory. Add half the rye flour and stir in the melted fat. Now add the rest of the rye flour, stirring with a large wooden spoon, and then beating vigorously until smooth (two minutes or so). Stir in the mixed whole wheat and white flours until you can't stir any more; resort to working the sticky, impossible-looking dough with your hands, sprinkling in only as much of the reserve flour as you need to make the dough ready for kneading. Turn out on a lightly floured surface and knead for about eight to 10 minutes, occasionally removing any film of dough which sticks to the board with a scraper, and re-dusting the board with flour. When smooth, form into a ball, roll around in a lightly greased bowl, cover and set in a warm place (80° to 85°F). Let rise until doubled in bulk—this will take 50 minutes or more.

Punch down in the bowl, and let rise another 10 minutes. Shape two round loaves, somewhat flattened. Place on a large greased baking sheet, leaving each loaf with as much room as possible. Cover, return to the warm place and let rise again for about 40 minutes. [*Preheat oven to 375°F.*] Now slash the tops, brush the surface with water or egg and bake for 30 to 45 minutes, or until done. Turn out and cool on a metal rack.

◦⟋ Minnesota Limpa ⟍◦

While we have Scandinavia to thank for this chewy, wonderful and surprising bread, we might never —except as tourists —have had much acquaintance with it were it not for the many Swedish and Norwegian settlers who came to Minnesota and North Dakota to farm in the middle of the 19th century. Recipe by A. C. Lind, Minnesota

Yields: Two round loaves

1 cup hot water
  (115° to 125°F)

⅓ cup brown sugar,
  firmly packed

¼ cup corn syrup, light
  or dark

2 tablespoons shortening
  or butter

2 tablespoons orange peel,
  coarsely grated

2 heaping tablespoons
  candied orange peel,
  chopped (optional)

1 teaspoon caraway seeds

1 teaspoon fennel seeds

½ teaspoon anise

1 teaspoon salt

2 envelopes dry yeast

½ cup warm water
  (105° to 115°F)

2½ cups rye flour

3 cups all-purpose flour

1 cup all-purpose flour
  (reserved)

 One greased baking sheet

In a large mixing bowl, stir the sugar, corn syrup and shortening into a cup of hot water, to dissolve and/or melt the ingredients. Add the orange peel (the candied peel is optional, but adds a wonderful chewiness), caraway, fennel and anise seeds, and the salt. Dissolve the yeast in a half cup of warm water and add to the other liquid. Now start adding the rye flour, beating hard with a wooden spoon, and then the all-purpose flour. Add only what you need of the reserve cup of flour to make a soft and workable dough. Turn out on a floured surface and knead for eight to 10 minutes until smooth and elastic. Grease the dough surface by rolling it in a greased bowl. Cover the bowl and put in a warm place (80° to 85°F) until the dough doubles its size. This will take about an hour and a half to two hours.

    Punch down and knead about six times before dividing the dough in half. Shape two loaves into slightly flattened rounds, and place on a greased baking sheet. Cover and let the loaves double in size in a warm place for about an hour. [*Preheat oven to 375°F.*] Bake for 30 to 40 minutes, or until done. This bread, by the way, will not sound very "hollow" when tapped on the bottom for doneness. Brush the tops right away with butter, and cool on a rack.

Notes: _____

_____

_____

_____

_____

_____

_____

Date first tried: _____

Notes: _____

_____

_____

_____

_____

_____

_____

Date first tried: _____

❧ Oatmaple Bread ❧

There's something very comforting about hot oatmeal, especially with lots of butter, maple syrup (or lumpy brown sugar) and milk. I look forward to sitting down with a big bowl of well-cooked oatmeal for supper some cold winter nights; I think about it all the way home. I like to sit on the sofa, bowl in my lap, a small book of short stories to read, and my cats looking forward eagerly to the lick of sweet stickiness that I'll leave on the spoon for them. Oatmaple Bread, served warmed with nothing but butter, has one great advantage—I don't have to wait for a cold night to eat it!

Yields: Two loaves

1½ cup uncooked rolled oats
  (quick oats are fine)
1 cup lowfat milk, added to
¾ cup water, scalded
¼ cup warm water
  (105° to 115°F)
1 envelope dry yeast
2 tablespoons butter
  or shortening

½ cup maple syrup
1 teaspoon salt
1 egg, lightly beaten
4 cups all-purpose flour
1 cup all-purpose flour
  (reserved)

 Two greased loaf pans, 8½″ x 4½″ x 2½″

In a large mixing bowl, slowly pour scalding milk and water mixture over uncooked oatmeal and stir. Mash any lumps that form. In a cup, proof the yeast in a quarter cup of warm water for five minutes. Stir butter, maple syrup and salt into the oatmeal mixture and let cool a bit before adding the yeast mixture. Too much heat will bedevil the yeast. Stir in the beaten egg and mix thoroughly. Now beat in the flour, a cup at a time, until the dough is soft and no longer sticky. You may not need the reserve cup of flour, but use as much as necessary to make the dough workable with your hands. Turn dough out on a floured surface, and knead for eight to 10 minutes until it is smooth and elastic. Roll the ball around in a greased bowl to coat the entire surface and cover. Let rise in a warm place (80° to 85°F) until it has doubled in bulk—at least an hour.

Punch down and return to the floured surface. Divide the dough in half and form two long ovals. Place the oval loaves in the greased pans, cover, and return to the warmth for a second doubling. This rising will not take as long as the first. [*Preheat oven to 350°F.*] Prepare the crust as desired (see page 10.) Now bake for 40 to 50 minutes, or until done. Cool in the pan for a few minutes before turning out on wire racks.

VARIATIONS: Before kneading, mix in ½ cup of chopped walnuts or chopped *hulled* sunflower seeds.

Notes:_____

_____

_____

_____

_____

_____

_____

Date first tried:_____

∽ Dilly Dally Bread ∼

This is another batter bread which you will love. The aroma of baking herb breads, especially those made with onion, is mouth-watering, and the taste is delicious. The name comes from the relatively short —half-hour —rising times: dilly-dallying time for the cook! This recipe was adapted from several sources by a woman whose hobby is herb-gardening. She often makes it with fresh basil (1 tablespoon, minced) or fresh marjoram (two rounded teaspoons, minced) instead of dill. Recipe by Martha Rayburn, Indiana

Yields: One loaf

1 envelope dry yeast
¼ cup warm water
   (105° to 115°F)
1 cup milk, scalded
1½ teaspoon light
   brown sugar
1 teaspoon salt
2 tablespoons butter
   or shortening

2 teaspoons fresh minced
   onion
1 tablespoon minced fresh
   dillweed
1 teaspoon celery seed
2½ cups all-purpose flour
½ cup all-purpose flour
   (reserved)
1 egg, lightly beaten

 One greased loaf pan, 9″ x 5″ x 3″

Dissolve yeast in warm water in a cup. Scald the milk in a saucepan, remove from the stove, and stir in sugar, salt, butter, onion (substitute 1 tablespoon instant minced onion if you wish), dill and celery seed until butter is melted. Put the flour in a good-sized mixing bowl and add the cooled milk mixture to it. Add the yeast and then the egg and beat for a minute with a big spoon to make a stiff batter. Cover the bowl and let batter double in bulk in a warm place (80° to 85°F). This should take 35 to 45 minutes.

Stir down and then spoon the batter into a greased loaf pan and spread evenly. Cover again and let rise for a half hour, until nearly doubled. [*Preheat oven to 350°F.*] Bake for 35 to 50 minutes, until loaf tests done. If the loaf is browning too quickly, cover it loosely with foil after 20 minutes or so. Turn out on a rack to cool and brush top with butter.

VARIATION: Bake Dilly Dally Bread in a greased ring mold (this will take 25 to 35 minutes), and turn out to cool on a rack. To serve, slice in two-inch wedges and serve on a large round platter with a dish of herbed butter (see page 90) or tuna salad in the center. This batter bread, like most batter breads, may also be baked in a well-greased casserole dish.

⤜ Monkey Bread ⤛

Everyone loves to eat Monkey Bread. It's not so much the taste, although that is very good, as the form: who could possibly resist pulling off their own bubbles of bread to eat? The peanuts are a surprise that children especially like. In fact, in tribute to their pleasure, another name for this recipe is Giggle Bread! LCF

Yields: One large loaf

2 envelopes dry yeast
¼ cup light brown sugar
½ cup warm water
　(105° to 115°F)
1¼ cup warm milk
　(105° to 115°F)
½ cup butter (1 stick)
3 eggs, lightly beaten

3 tablespoons creamy
　peanut butter
6 cups all-purpose flour
1 cup all-purpose flour
　(reserved)
¼ to ½ cup dry roasted
　peanuts

 One greased 10″ tube pan

Stir the yeast and sugar into the warm water in a large mixing bowl. Heat the milk in a saucepan, remove from the stove, and stir in the butter. Add to the yeast mixture. Now stir in the eggs and peanut butter, and beat briskly with a wooden spoon about 15 strokes to blend thoroughly. Add the flour, a cup at a time, stirring well. You may not need the reserve cup. The dough will be quite sticky, but as soon as it seems possible to handle it, turn out on a floured surface. Knead for eight to 10 minutes until smooth and elastic, dusting the hands with flour as necessary. Roll the dough ball in a buttered bowl and cover with a dish towel or plastic wrap. Place in a warm spot (80° to 85°F) for an hour to rise. When doubled in bulk, punch down and let rest for five minutes. Lightly flour the board again and put the dough on it. Now you may either pinch off dough to form balls the size of golf balls, or cut the dough in half, over and over, to get 32 pieces. While forming the balls in your palms, insert a surprise peanut in each. Arrange half the balls in a greased tube pan. They may or may not touch. The rest of the balls form the second layer. Don't worry about gaps—these are filled when the loaf rises. Cover and let dough rise again for about 40 minutes, until doubled in bulk. [*Preheat oven to 375°F.*] Bake for 30 to 40 minutes, or until done. Turn out on a rack to cool. Serve upside down if you like.

VARIATION: If you would like to add to the fun, put a peanut in only one ball—with a prize of some sort for the winner.

Notes: _____

_____

_____

_____

_____

_____

_____

_____

Date first tried: _____

Notes:_____

_____

_____

_____

_____

_____

_____

Date first tried:_____

~ Lois' Bread ~

This excellent toasting bread is made with a "sponge"—a fermented mixture of the yeast, sugar and part of the dry ingredients. Many 18th and 19th century bread recipes called for sponges. Recipe contributed by Lois Douglass, Virginia

Yields: Two loaves

2 envelopes dry yeast

2 teaspoons granulated sugar

½ cup warm water
  (105° to 115°F)

2 cups warm buttermilk
  (105° to 115°F)

1 egg, slightly beaten

½ cup rolled oats
  (quick oatmeal is fine)

½ cup wheat germ
  (raw or toasted)

½ cup cornmeal

½ cup instant mashed
  potatoes (dry)

2 teaspoons salt

½ cup blackstrap molasses

4 cups all-purpose flour

1 cup all-purpose flour
  (reserved)

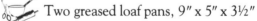 Two greased loaf pans, 9″ x 5″ x 3½″

In a small bowl, dissolve sugar and yeast in warm water. Warm the buttermilk, pour into a good-sized mixing bowl, and stir in the beaten egg. Add all the dry ingredients except the all-purpose flour, and then stir in the yeast mixture. Set this sponge aside in a warm, draft-free place for 45 to 50 minutes to rise. In a large mixing bowl, put four cups of all-purpose flour. Make a "well" in the flour and pour in the sponge. Add the molasses. With a big wooden spoon, beat the mixture until it is of kneading consistency. This will take a minute or two. Turn dough out on a floured surface and knead until it is satiny and elastic. Divide in half, form two loaves, and put each into a greased loaf pan. Cover and put in a warm place (80° to 85°F) until the loaves have doubled in bulk. This will take 45 minutes to an hour. [*Preheat oven to 350°F.*] When loaves are ready, place in oven and lower temperature at once to 325°F. Bake about 45 minutes, or until loaves test done. Turn out on a rack to cool.

⇒ Anadama Bread ⇐

Unlike most cornbreads, which are fairly crumbly and get their rise out of baking powder or buttermilk and soda, Anadama Bread is rather chewy and is made with yeast. The name is a mystery which many food writers have tried to solve. Most common is the angry husband theory, "Anna, dammit . . ." but I'm convinced that somehow the explanation lies in a Greek dictionary. Ana-, as a Greek prefix, means up, and this is a risen bread. That doesn't explain dama, however. Perhaps the bread was first made in a tube pan or as a free-form woven "wreath," and got its name from anadema *the Greek word for wreath or chaplet.*

Yields: Two loaves

3½ cups all-purpose flour

2 cups all-purpose flour
   (reserved)

2 envelopes dry yeast

1 cup cornmeal (yellow
   or white)

2 cups boiling water

½ cup dark molasses

⅓ cup margarine, butter or
   shortening

2 teaspoons salt

 Two greased loaf pans, 8½" x 4½" x 2½"

In a large mixing bowl, combine about two cups of flour and dry yeast, and set aside. Boil two cups of water in a two-quart saucepan and remove from heat. Slowly and constantly stir one cup of cornmeal into the water, making sure that no lumps form. Then add the molasses, shortening and salt. Combine the still warm cornmeal mixture with the flour and yeast. Beat at low speed with an electric mixer for about two minutes, or vigorously by hand for five minutes. Stir in by hand enough of the remainder of the flour (dipping into the reserve if necessary) for a thick batter, which stiffens to a soft dough with mixing.

Turn the dough out onto a lightly floured surface and knead for seven or eight minutes. When smooth and elastic, put dough in a lightly greased bowl, turning the ball until the entire surface is greased. Cover and put the bowl in a warm spot (80° to 85°F) for about an hour until the dough doubles in bulk. Remove dough from bowl and punch down. Cut in half, cover, and let the dough rest for 10 minutes. Then shape into oblong pieces about 8½" long, to touch both ends of the pans, and place in greased loaf pans. Cover and return to a warm place for about 45 minutes. [*Preheat oven to 375°F.*] When the loaves have again doubled in bulk, bake about 40 minutes, or until done. Remove from pans and cool on a metal rack.

Notes: _____

_____

_____

_____

_____

_____

_____

_____

Date first tried: _____

THE STERLING DID IT

ONLY ONE FIRE POT OF COAL

ONLY ONE BBL. OF FLOUR

BAKED IN 10 HOURS

ONLY 231 LOAVES

"HAS NO EQUAL"

Copyright 1895 by
SILL STOVE WORKS, ROCHESTER, N.Y.

"SEE OUR RECORD ON OTHER SIDE"

THE experiment of baking one barrel of flour into 231 loaves of well-baked bread (1¼ lbs. of dough each) in our New STERLING RANGE, with a minimum quantity of coal, in the least possible time, was first done at our works January 8th of this year. The picture on the opposite side is an exact illustration of the photograph taken after the baking, with results as stated, **proving beyond a doubt that the combined, patented, constructive features** (exclusively our own and used only in the new STERLING) **are unequaled by any other Range in the world, no matter of what material it is made, in what section of the country it is manufactured, or how much more it may cost than ours.**

With the assistance of several of our customers we have given several additional baking exhibits, and not only have we **broken our first record many times** but we have practically demonstrated the fact that the STERLING RANGE really **HAS NO EQUAL.**

Just stop to think of it—*a whole barrel of flour baked into bread in less than ten hours and with less than ten cents worth of fuel.* Can you do better than buy a New STERLING RANGE?

Salt-Rising Bread

This is probably one of the most difficult breads to make. The taste and texture are so distinctive, however, that it is worth giving it a try. Most people use cornmeal to make the sponge, but raw, thinly sliced potatoes are sometimes used too. If you try it with potatoes, new ones are best. Use one cup of potato slices and the rest of the recipe is the same, except that before mixing the sponge with the rest of the ingredients put the sponge in cheesecloth, squeeze the liquid out and discard the potato slices.

Yields: Two loaves

½ cup cornmeal

1 tablespoon sugar

½ teaspoon salt

1 cup sweet milk, scalded

1 tablespoon sugar

2 tablespoons shortening

1 teaspoon salt

1 cup warm water
(100° to 110°F)

4 cups all-purpose flour

½ cup all-purpose flour
(reserved)

Notes: _____

_____

_____

_____

_____

_____

_____

Date first tried:_____

 Two greased loaf pans, 8½" x 4½" x 2½"

In a warmed ceramic mixing bowl, put the cornmeal, a tablespoon of sugar and a half teaspoon of salt. Pour in a cup of scalded milk (just short of boiling) and stir. Cover the bowl and put in a warm place (90° to 100°F), warmer than that warm spot you have found for the yeast breads. Leave to ferment for six to seven hours, or even longer—overnight or all day. When the mixture is light and foamy, with a sweetish odor, it is ready. If nothing has happened, you'll have to start over from scratch.

In a large mixing bowl, put one tablespoon of sugar, a teaspoon of salt, the shortening and two cups, roughly, of the flour. Add the fermented cornmeal mixture. Beat thoroughly about 75 to 100 strokes. Set the covered bowl in a basin (a dishwashing pan is good) of hot water (115°F), or back in the warm spot. Keep replenishing the hot water in the basin if you use that method. After about two hours, the sponge will be very light and bubbly.

Grease a large warmed mixing bowl (ceramic holds the heat much better than stainless steel; plastic is neutral and stays at room temperature), and put the sponge in it. Now stir in two more cups of flour, or enough to make a soft dough. Turn out on a floured surface and knead for eight to 10 minutes. Divide the dough in half, shape loaves, and place in well-greased loaf pans. Cover the pans and let rise in a warm place until doubled in bulk. This will take about an hour. [*Preheat oven to 350°F.*] Bake 45 minutes, or until done. Turn out on a rack to cool.

⮜ Spotted Dog ⮞
SODA BREAD

A collector of recipes and cookbooks, who babysat for my brother and me when we were small, shares this "way back when" recipe with all of us. It was used by her mother, Mary Lawlor Fischer, for many years and the bread was baked every St. Patrick's Day. An Irish cousin of Rose Mary's wrote that it is called "Spotted Dog" if candied fruit is added instead of raisins. We couldn't resist giving you this version! Recipe contributed by Rose Mary Fischer, Ohio

Yields: One large round loaf

4 cups all-purpose flour	1½ cups buttermilk
1 teaspoon baking soda	1 tablespoon caraway seeds
2 teaspoons baking powder	½ cup candied fruit, cut up
1 teaspoon salt	2 tablespoons sugar
2 tablespoons margarine or shortening	2 tablespoons water
½ cup sugar	

 One greased baking sheet

Mix flour, baking soda and powder, and salt together in a large mixing bowl. Rub the shortening into this mixture. Mix in the sugar. Add the buttermilk and stir to make a dough. Add the caraway seeds and the candied fruit (or an equal amout of raisins). Knead two or three minutes and shape into a round flattened loaf, about 2½" thick. [*Preheat oven to 375°F.*] Place on a greased baking sheet. With a wet knife, score a cross on top, about half an inch deep, going from edge to edge. These score marks keep the loaf from cracking, and also make it easy to divide into quarters. Bake for 60 to 65 minutes, or until it tests done with a wooden toothpick. At about 50 minutes, mix a glaze of two tablespoons each of sugar and water, and brush the mixture on top of the loaf. When done, turn out and cool on a rack.

Old-Timers' Sourdough Bread

If you want to be a little more new-timer, sourdough starter is sold, ready-made, in ceramic containers. But it isn't very difficult to make, and you can store it in the refrigerator for about two weeks before the ingredients need to be replenished (with equal amounts of flour and water) and re-fermented in a warm spot for 12 hours. Sourdough bread is identified with Old West prospectors, sheepherders and settlers. A successful starter could be carried around, used, and replenished, practically forever. A nickname for crusty old prospectors was "sourdough."

Yields: Two loaves

1 envelope dry yeast

3 cups warm water
(105° to 115°F)

3 cups all-purpose flour

1 cup warm water
(105° to 115°F)

1 envelope dry yeast

1½ cups sourdough starter,
stirred and at room
temperature

2 tablespoons honey
(or sugar or molasses)

1½ teaspoons salt

2 eggs, lightly beaten

3 tablespoons butter,
softened

4 cups all-purpose flour

2 cups all-purpose flour
(reserved)

 Two greased loaf pans, 8½″ x 4½″ x 2½″

To make the starter, mix one envelope of yeast, and three cups each of flour and warm water in a large mixing bowl. Cover with a splatter screen or cheesecloth (nothing less porous), and put in a warm place (80° to 85°F) for at least 48 hours. This mixture will, if everything goes well, become bubbly and gaseous. If not, discard and start over. The longer it ferments, the sourer it becomes. Stir occasionally. If the mixture begins to dry out, add more warm water.

To make the bread, take another large mixing bowl and dissolve another envelope of yeast in a cup of warm water. Proof for five minutes. Add the room temperature sourdough starter, honey, salt, eggs, butter and four cups of flour. Beat the batter well. Cover the bowl with a damp dishtowel and put in a warm spot (80° to 85°F) to double in bulk. This takes about 90 minutes or so. Add enough of the reserve flour to make a soft dough. [*Add more flour here to make a stiff dough if you are going to make free-form loaves.*] Turn out on a floured surface and knead for eight to 10 minutes until smooth and elastic. Cut in half and shape into two loaves. Place in greased loaf pans, slash the tops, brush with butter, cover, and let rise until doubled in bulk. This takes 60 to 90 minutes. [*Preheat oven to 375°F.*] Bake for 40 to 50 minutes, or until done. Turn out on rack to cool.

Notes: _____

_____

_____

_____

_____

_____

_____

Date first tried: _____

∽ Curried Olive Nut Bread ∽

This is a quick bread with a wonderfully unusual flavor. It is good for canapés or small sandwiches, and lends itself to experimenting with spreads and toppings. Try a mix of cream cheese, grated sharp Cheddar cheese and crumbled bacon.

Yields: One loaf

1 cup stuffed green olives, drained and sliced

1 teaspoon curry powder

1 teaspoon minced onion flakes

2 tablespoons corn oil

1½ cups all-purpose flour

4 teaspoons baking powder

½ teaspoon salt

1 cup whole wheat flour

1 egg, well-beaten

1 cup milk

1 cup walnuts or pecans, chopped

 One greased loaf pan, 8½" x 4½" x 2½"

A day before breadmaking, mix the green olives, onion, curry powder and corn oil in a small bowl. Put in the refrigerator, and stir well a number of times—say every time you visit the kitchen during the evening. The marinated olives will absorb the curry and onion flavors.

In a good sized bowl, sift the flour, salt and baking powder and add the whole wheat flour. [*Preheat oven to 350°F.*] Mix the egg and milk, and stir quickly into flour mixture. Try to keep your stirring down to 15 strokes. Stir in the olives, with bits of minced onion, and the chopped nuts. Put mixture into a greased loaf pan and bake for about 45 minutes, or until done. Turn out to cool on a rack. Do not slice until thoroughly cool.

Nutty Cheese Quick Bread

This bread smells so good that your loaf may not last long enough to cool! Substitutions are possible, as usual. Sharp Cheddar has the most punch, but if you've got nothing but some old Romano and mild Cheddar in the fridge, use them. You may also leave out the vegetable juice: in that case, use only 2½ cups of flour. If you don't have buttermilk, use soured milk, or add a teaspoon of lemon juice to a cup of sweet milk.

Yields: One loaf

3¼ cups all-purpose flour

2 teaspoons baking powder

1 teaspoon salt (optional)

½ teaspoon dry mustard

½ teaspoon baking soda

1 dash cayenne pepper

¼ cup shortening (½ stick butter or margarine)

1 cup sharp Cheddar cheese, grated

1 teaspoon steak sauce (Worcestershire, HP, A-1, etc.)

1 cup buttermilk

¼ cup tomato or vegetable juice

1 tablespoon molasses

1 cup walnuts, chopped

 One greased loaf pan, 9″ x 4½″ x 3½″

Sift flour, baking powder and soda, salt, mustard and cayenne pepper in a large mixing bowl. Work in the shortening with a pastry blender or rub in with your fingers. Stir in cheese. [*Preheat oven to 350°F.*] In another bowl, combine liquids and stir quickly into flour mixture. Don't overmix. Stir in the chopped nuts. Turn the batter into a greased loaf pan, spreading out evenly with a rubber spatula. Bake 45 to 60 minutes, depending on your oven. As with all breads that contain cheese, keep a close watch after 20 minutes or so to be sure that the top is not browning too quickly, or even burning. Cover loosely with foil if necessary. When done, turn out on a rack to cool. If you want to eat this bread warm, do not try to slice too thinly.

Notes: _____
_____
_____
_____
_____
_____
_____
_____

Date first tried:_____

 Orange Bread

Not one to stick to someone else's recipe, I adapted this orange bread from several sources, including James Beard's Lemon Bread recipe. I first made it for a Christmas party, and had bought a number of oranges to use in making a fabulous cranberry sauce. All those oranges appealed to my imagination. This is a dense moist bread with a lovely flavor. I eat it like cake. LCF

Yields: One loaf

1 orange rind, grated
1 orange rind, trimmed of
   white and minced
water to cover
½ cup sugar
½ cup butter (1 stick)
2 eggs, lightly beaten

½ cup thawed orange juice
   concentrate
1 cup milk
2¼ cups all-purpose flour
3 teaspoons baking powder
1 teaspoon salt
¼ cup pecans, chopped

 One greased loaf pan, 8½″ x 4½″ x 2½″

Stew the grated and minced orange rind in a small saucepan, in barely enough water to cover, for five minutes. Let cool to room temperature. In a large mixing bowl, cream the butter and sugar. Mix in the orange rind. Stir in the eggs, one at a time, beating hard. Stir in the orange juice concentrate and the milk. Put half the flour in a large sifter, then the salt and baking powder, then the rest of the flour. Sift a third of the dry ingredients into the liquid mixture and stir thoroughly. Add another third and stir. [*Preheat oven to 350°F.*] Put the final third of flour in, and then nuts, and beat 15 to 20 vigorous strokes. Vigorous beating for any length of time increases the cakiness of the bread, which makes it harder to slice and eat like bread. Turn into a greased and flour-dusted loaf pan. Bake about 50 minutes until done. Turn out on a rack to cool thoroughly. Wrap securely and store overnight. Do not try to slice until the next day.

Notes: _____
_____
_____
_____
_____
_____
_____
_____

Date first tried: _____

Notes:_____

_____

_____

_____

_____

Date first tried:_____

MARZIPAN CARROTS

This recipe will make enough marzipan for a good handful of small carrots. If you'd like to make more, simply double the recipe. In blender or food processor blend ¾ cup of blanched almonds, ¼ cup of orange juice, and ⅓ cup of granulated sugar to make an almond paste. Remove from blender and put in mixing bowl. Add one cup of confectioners' sugar and 1½ teaspoons of rosewater. Rub ingredients together with your fingers, turn out on a cool marble slab and knead for 15 to 20 minutes. Take ⅛ of the paste for the leaves. Form miniature carrots with the remainder, rolling in your palms. Roll out tiny "straws" for stems. Dry for an hour on a rack, then mark the carrots with realistic little depressions, using the back of a knife. Let a real carrot be your guide. Using vegetable colorings, dye the carrots by dipping (or painting with a small brush). Let dry on the rack, then store in an airtight container in the refrigerator, or place directly on cooled carrot bread.

⤚ Chloe's 24k Carrot Bread ⤙

Lest you are scared off this one, "24k" stands for the quality of the bread, not the number of carrots needed. Actually, I didn't know whether to call it 24k Chloe's Carrot Bread or the way I've got it here–Chloe is my beloved dog. I especially like making this bread because Chloe loves raw carrots, and waits eagerly for those inch-long stubs which I dare not try to grate. LCF

Yields: Two medium loaves

2 cups all-purpose flour
2 teaspoons baking soda
1 teaspoon baking powder
1 teaspoon cinnamon
½ teaspoon salt
¼ teaspoon ginger
1 cup light brown sugar
2 eggs, well-beaten
½ cup oil (peanut, safflower or corn)
1 teaspoon vanilla extract
2 cups raw carrots, grated
1 cup pecans or walnuts, chopped, or
1 cup hulled sunflower seeds, raw

 Two greased loaf pans, 8½″ x 4½″ x 2½″

In a large mixing bowl, sift the flour, baking powder, soda, cinnamon, ginger and salt together. Combine the sugar, eggs, oil and vanilla, and stir into the flour mixture. [*Preheat oven to 350°F.*] Blend in the carrots and nuts (or seeds) with a few swift and thorough strokes. With a rubber spatula, put batter into the greased loaf pans; spread evenly around. Bake for about an hour, until bread tests done (see page 10). Invert pans on rack and cool for five to 10 minutes before removing the pans. When thoroughly cooled, wrap in foil or waxed paper and keep a day before slicing. This bread can also be baked in an 8″ x 8″ x 2″ baking dish, and served hot in big squares. Try it with lemon ice cream for dessert!

SERVING SUGGESTION: Frost cooled bread with sifted confectioners' sugar and decorate with marzipan carrots.

∼ Too-Many-Zucchinis Bread ∼

This recipe is an adaptation of one sent by Mrs. E. C. Hobbitt of California to Gourmet, back in 1974 when zucchinis started over-breeding! Doesn't it seem to you in retrospect that it wasn't too many years ago when the zucchini population was not anything to worry about? Anyway, the treasury of American home cooking has plenty of excellent recipes for the tasty green squash.

Yields: Two loaves

3 eggs, well-beaten
1 cup sugar
1 cup cooking oil
1 tablespoon vanilla extract
2 cups zucchini, coarsely grated
1 lemon rind, grated
2 cups all-purpose flour

1 tablespoon cinnamon
1 teaspoon cardamon
2 teaspoons baking soda
1 teaspoon salt
¼ teaspoon baking powder
1 cup walnuts or pecans,
   chopped or broken

Notes: _____

_____

_____

_____

_____

_____

_____

_____

Date first tried: _____

 Two greased and floured loaf pans, 8½″ x 4½″ x 3″

Beat the eggs in a large bowl until light and frothy. Add the sugar, oil and vanilla and beat well. The mixture should be thick and lemon colored. Stir in the zucchini and grated lemon rind. Sift in the flour, spices, baking soda, baking powder and salt. [*Preheat oven to 350°F.*] Stir well. Fold in the chopped nuts. Spoon the batter into the greased and flour-dusted loaf pans, filling each about two-thirds full. Bake for about an hour, or until a cake tester or broomstraw comes out dry. Cool in the pans for about 10 minutes, then turn out on a rack to cool thoroughly before slicing.

꒱Peter Pumpkin Bread꒱

"When the frost is on the punkin" I am especially thankful for living in the United States where pumpkins are considered human food, not pig food! Use either canned pumpkin (not the pie mixture) or steam your own pumpkin chunks. You can also make similar breads with other cooked mashed squashes, or with mashed sweet potatoes. Each version is a bit different in flavor, but they're all good.

Yields: One loaf

1 cup brown sugar, firmly
   packed
½ cup shortening
2 eggs
2 cups cooked, mashed
   pumpkin (cooled)
½ cup milk
2 cups all-purpose flour
2 teaspoons baking powder

½ teaspoon salt
1 teaspoon ground cinnamon
½ teaspoon ground nutmeg
¼ teaspoon powdered ginger
¼ teaspoon ground cloves
¼ teaspoon baking soda
¾ cup walnuts, chopped

 One greased loaf pan, 9″ x 5″ x 3″

In a large mixing bowl, combine the sugar, shortening, eggs and pumpkin, and beat well. Mix the dry ingredients, except for the nuts. Stir a third of the dry ingredients into the pumpkin mixture, then half the milk, then another third of the flour, the rest of the milk, and the remaining flour and spices. Mix well and fold in the nuts. [*Preheat oven to 350°F.*] Pour batter into a greased loaf pan and spread evenly with a spatula. Bake for about an hour, or until done. Invert on rack and cool for 10 minutes before lifting off pan.

*Notes:*_____

_____

_____

_____

_____

_____

_____

*Date first tried:*_____

❧ Cranberry Bread ❧

"One of the most enjoyable activities since retiring to Cape Cod is gathering our own cranberries after the harvest is over. It's absolutely amazing how many of the dark rich red gems can be gleaned from along the edges of the ditches. Of course there are a few hazards, such as getting scratched by blackberry vines and getting wet by falling into a ditch! Red juice stains the knees of our jeans, but the beauty of the bogs on a fine October day compensates for any discomfort. This bread recipe is from the late Helen Tryon, a home economist at the school where my husband was principal."
Recipe contributed by Dot and Jack Roberts, Massachusetts

Yields: One loaf

2 cups sifted all-purpose
   flour
1 cup sugar
2 teaspoons baking powder
½ teaspoon baking soda
½ teaspoon salt
2 tablespoons shortening
½ cup orange juice
1 orange rind, grated
½ cup boiling water
1 egg, beaten
1 cup pecans or walnuts,
   chopped or broken
1 cup cranberries, cut in
   pieces or halves

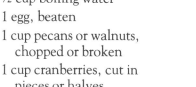

 One greased loaf pan, 9″ x 5″ x 3″

Sift flour and sugar with baking powder, soda and salt into a bowl. Sift three times. Boil a half-cup of water. In a measuring cup, put the shortening and the orange juice plus enough boiling water to make seven-eighths of a cup. Mix in the grated orange rind and let sit for five minutes to steep and cool. Put the orange mixture into a large mixing bowl and add the egg. Stir in the dry ingredients, mixing thoroughly but without overbeating. Add the nutmeats and the cranberry pieces. [*Preheat oven to 350°F.*] Spoon batter into a greased loaf pan. Bake for 45 to 60 minutes, testing with a tester or wooden toothpick at 45 minutes. Leave in pan for 15 to 20 minutes to cool, then turn out on a rack.

Notes: _____
_____
_____
_____
_____
_____
_____
_____

Date first tried: _____

Notes:_____

_____

_____

_____

_____

_____

_____

Date first tried:_____

～ Caraway Bread ～

This is a very nicely flavored tea bread. It is also good when cut in thick slices, spread with butter and toasted in a broiler oven. Serve with poached eggs and bacon for a new brunch treat. Recipe contributed by Mary Mac Franklin, Virginia.

Yields: One loaf

¼ cup butter (½ stick)   1 tablespoon baking powder
¾ cup sugar   ¾ cup milk
1 egg, well-beaten   ¾ teaspoon vanilla
1⅔ cups all-purpose flour   1 tablespoon caraway seeds
¼ teaspoon salt

 One greased and lightly floured loaf pan,
8½" x 4½" x 2½"

Cream the butter and sugar in a good-sized mixing bowl. Add the egg. Sift a third of the flour, baking powder and salt together, into the creamed mixture. Combine the milk and vanilla. Stir half the milk mixture into the creamed mix. Stir in another third of the dry ingredients, the rest of the milk, then the last third of flour. Don't overwork or the bread will be too finely crumbed. [*Preheat oven to 350°F.*] Stir in the caraway seeds. Turn into a buttered and flour-dusted loaf pan. Lightly sprinkle the top with sugar. Bake for 30 to 40 minutes until done. Cool for five minutes in the pan and then turn out onto a rack to cool.

❦ Mott Haven Banana Bread ❧

With new cookbooks arriving all the time, and old ones sitting on the shelves practically begging to be dipped into and savored, it is no wonder that many librarians have very extensive collections of recipes. This recipe, which came from a now-unidentifiable book, was first shared among the librarians at New York's Mott Haven branch in 1936. It makes a lovely dense bread which can be sliced very thin and spread with butter, or eaten in chunks. Recipe contributed by Mary Mac Franklin, Virginia

Yields: One loaf

¾ cup sugar
½ cup butter (1 stick)
2 eggs, beaten
3 large or 4 small bananas,
    well-mashed
1¾ cups all-purpose flour
1 teaspoon baking soda
dash of salt

 One greased loaf pan, 8 ½" x 4 ½" x 2 ½"

In a good-sized mixing bowl, cream the butter and sugar until they are smooth and pale. Add the beaten eggs and the mashed bananas and mix thoroughly with a fork. [*Preheat oven to 350°F.*] Sift the flour, soda and salt together and stir into the liquid mixture. Do not over-stir. With a rubber spatula, put the batter in a greased loaf pan, pushing it out evenly into the corners. Bake for about 50 minutes, or until the top splits slightly and a cake tester or broomstraw stuck into the center comes out dry. Let the bread cool for five minutes in the pan, then turn out on a metal cooling rack.

Notes: _____

_____
_____
_____
_____
_____
_____
_____

Date first tried: _____

❧ Gingerbread ❧

Gingerbread smells heavenly while it's baking. It used to be served with meals, rather than as a dessert as it is so often served now. Try hot gingerbread, cut in hunks and buttered, with chicken or vegetable dinners.

Yields: One pan

½ cup sugar
½ cup shortening (strained
  bacon fat, lard or butter)
1 tablespoon vegetable oil
1 cup molasses
¾ cup boiling water
2 teaspoons baking soda
2 cups all-purpose flour
1 heaping teaspoon powdered
  ginger

1 teaspoon ground cloves
1 teaspoon cinnamon
1 dash cayenne pepper
½ teaspoon salt (not needed
  with bacon fat)
2 eggs, well-beaten

 One greased pan, 9″ x 9″ x 2″

In a large mixing bowl, cream the sugar and the shortening and oil, then stir in the molasses. Dissolve the soda in the boiling water and add to the sweet mixture. Sift the flour and spices and beat into liquid mixture. Stir in the eggs. [*Preheat oven to 350°F.*] Spoon batter into the greased pan and bake for about 35 to 45 minutes until it pulls away from the sides and is springy to the touch. Cut into squares while hot. Serve with butter.

SERVING VARIATION Serve as dessert with warm lemon sauce, made as follows. In a small double boiler, mix 1 cup of boiling water, ½ cup of sugar, and 1 tablespoon of cornstarch or arrowroot, and stir constantly for five minutes until thickened and smooth. Remove from stove and stir in 3 tablespoons of sweet butter, 1½ tablespoons of lemon juice, the grated rind of one lemon, a dash of nutmeg and a dash of salt.

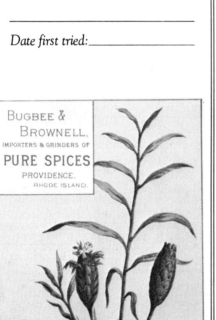

BUGBEE &
BROWNELL,
IMPORTERS & GRINDERS OF
PURE SPICES
PROVIDENCE.
RHODE ISLAND.

GINGER

Notes: _____

_____

_____

_____

_____

_____

_____

_____

Date first tried: _____

∽ Tea Scones ∽

Scones, pronounced something like "scuns," are one of the most famous foods of Scotland. Traditionally they are cooked on a griddle, over the heat source, and served in wedges with lots and lots of butter and jam.

Yields: Two 6″ circles, which can be cut
into four, six or eight wedges

2 cups all-purpose flour
2 tablespoons sugar
½ teaspoon salt
3 teaspoons baking powder
⅓ cup butter or margarine
2 eggs, well-beaten
½ cup sweet milk or half-and-half
splash of sweet milk
granulated sugar

 One very, very lightly buttered baking sheet

Into a good-sized mixing bowl, sift the dry ingredients. Cut in the butter with a pastry blender until dough resembles coarse pea-sized crumbs. Add the eggs and milk and stir to make a soft dough with *lumps left in.* Do not overmix. Turn out on flour-dusted surface, divide in half, and knead each ball gently five or six times. [*Preheat oven to 400°– 425°F.*] Flatten by pushing or rolling into circles a half-inch thick. Trim into even circles with a small mixing bowl as guide, and shape leftover scraps into a "cook's scone;" or, leave edges rough as is. Now either score or mark wedges with a floured knife, or cut wedges all the way through. Brush tops with milk and lightly sprinkle with granulated sugar. Arrange scored circles or wedges (with space left between each wedge) on a baking sheet which has been very lightly buttered. Bake for 12 to 15 minutes until golden brown. Serve hot.

Notes: _____
_____
_____
_____
_____
_____
_____
_____

Date first tried: _____

Notes:_____

_____

_____

_____

_____

_____

_____

Date first tried:_____

SALLY LUN

Let over the fire till milk warm a pint of cream then take it off and put in 2 dessert spoonfuls of bleached barm*, the yolks of 3 eggs well beaten, pour the cream very easy on the eggs and keep it stirring that the eggs should not curdle, then strain it thro' a hair sieve with as much flour as will make it stiff dough, let it stand 2 hours to rise, then roll them in cakes what size you like and bake it if you have no cream put 1 oz butter in a pint of milk—

ANOTHER SALLY LUN

¼ the Butter melted in a pint warm milk, 3 eggs well beaten a tea cup of bleached barm, put to a pottle* flour mix them well together, it must lie 3 hours to rise 1 hour to bake it, it must be baked in a tin pan, when buttered put it in the pan cover it and let it lie 10 minutes.

From a manuscript "Cookery Book" begun January 27, 1831 in New Orleans. Lent by Kate Wyckoff, New York

(*Barm is malt liquor yeast; and a pottle is an old-time liquid measure equalling two quarts.)

⋙ Sally Lunn ⋘

There are several stories about the origin of the name of this nice bread. I think the prettiest by far is the theory that because the golden top crust and the white bottom evoke the sun and moon, the French words soleil et lune *form the original name — "Sally Lunn" being a phonetic English approximation. Anyway, the taste is heavenly enough to deserve the French appellation! This is only one of many Sally Lunn recipes, some of which date back 300 years in the South. Recipe contributed by Beatrice Huckaby, Virginia.*

Yields: One loaf

1 envelope dry yeast
¼ cup warm water
  (105° to 115°F)
½ cup butter (1 stick)
⅓ cup sugar
3 eggs
¾ cup milk, (105° to 115°F)
2½ cups all-purpose flour
1 teaspoon salt
1½ cup flour (reserved)

One well-buttered 10″ tube pan

In a cup, dissolve the yeast in warm water. In a large mixing bowl, cream the butter and sugar for about two minutes, then beat in one egg at a time. Add the milk, and then beat in a cup of the flour and salt mixture. Add the yeast, and then beat in the rest of the flour. You may not need any of the reserve flour. You are aiming to get a *stiff batter*; it won't be the same as a kneaded dough and will be sticky. Cover the bowl with a dish towel or plastic wrap and put in a warm place (80° to 85°F). The batter will double in bulk in about an hour.

Turn into a well-greased tube pan or two-quart Turk's-head mold, and push it out evenly with a rubber spatula. Cover and let rise again for 50 to 60 minutes. [*Preheat oven to 350°F.*] Bake for about 40 to 50 minutes until done. Test with a toothpick or cake tester, instead of turning it out and knocking on the bottom. This bread is somewhat fragile at first. When done, remove from the mold carefully: put a plate over the top, invert the mold and tap the loaf out. Use another plate to turn the loaf upright, and then slide it onto a metal rack to cool.

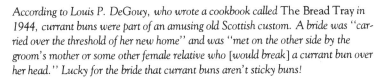 Strewn Currant Buns

According to Louis P. DeGouy, who wrote a cookbook called The Bread Tray *in 1944, currant buns were part of an amusing old Scottish custom. A bride was "carried over the threshold of her new home" and was "met on the other side by the groom's mother or some other female relative who [would break] a currant bun over her head." Lucky for the bride that currant buns aren't sticky buns!*

Yields: Eighteen to 22 buns

1 envelope dry yeast
¼ teaspoon sugar
½ cup warm water
   (105° to 115°F)
1 cup sweet milk, scalded
¼ cup butter or shortening
½ teaspoon salt
¼ teaspoon ground nutmeg
1 lemon rind, grated
2 eggs, unbeaten

2 tablespoons light brown
   sugar
2 tablespoons honey
¼ cup toasted wheat germ
3 cups all-purpose flour
1 cup all-purpose flour
   (reserved)
⅓ cup currants, soaked and
   patted dry

 One greased baking sheet

Dissolve yeast and a quarter-teaspoon of sugar in a half cup of warm water. Scald a cup of sweet milk (that's just short of boiling), remove from stove, and stir in butter, two tablespoons of sugar, honey, salt, nutmeg and lemon rind. When cooled to lukewarm, put mixture in large mixing bowl and beat in the eggs. Stir in the dissolved yeast and wheat germ and blend thoroughly. Sift in three cups of flour, beating sturdily all the while. Add as much of the reserved flour as needed to make a soft dough. Roll dough around in a buttered bowl, cover, and put in a warm place (80° to 85°F) until doubled in bulk, about 70 to 80 minutes.

Turn out on floured surface, punch down, and push into a large flattish disc. Strew the currants evenly around the surface and knead for two minutes, sifting a bit of flour on when necessary. Shape by hand into about 18 buns. Or roll out to half-inch thickness on a floured surface, and cut with a large floured biscuit cutter into about 20 buns. Place buns an inch apart on a greased baking sheet and cover loosely with a towel. Let rise in your warm place for 45 to 60 minutes, until doubled in bulk again. [*Preheat oven to 400°F.*] Bake until golden brown and serve hot, or warm, with butter and marmalade.

Notes: _____
_____
_____
_____
_____
_____
_____
_____

Date first tried: _____

⌁ Cottage Cheese Casserole Bread ⌁

This batter bread is practically a meal in itself. Try it with parsley or minced chives instead of dill, or with any combination of sweet or savory herbs, fresh or dried, that you like. Because I love cottage cheese and pineapple, I made it once with a quarter cup of canned pineapple pieces (not chunks), and added extra flour to compensate for the extra liquid. I left in the dill and onion and I thought it was wonderful—a real surprise.

Yields: One or two loaves, depending on your casserole

1 envelope dry yeast

¼ cup warm water
(105° to 115°F)

1 cup warmed cottage cheese,
creamed style
(105° to 115°F)

1 tablespoon butter or
margarine

2 tablespoons honey

¼ teaspoon baking soda

1 tablespoon minced onion
flakes or grated fresh onion

2 teaspoons dill seeds

1 teaspoon celery seeds

1 teaspoon salt

2¼ cups all-purpose flour

¼ cup all-purpose flour
(reserved)

1 egg

 One well-greased casserole dish, 1½-quart capacity

Proof the yeast in warm water. In a large mixing bowl, combine the heated cottage cheese, butter, honey, baking soda, onion, dill, celery seeds and salt. Stir in the flour, using the reserve if needed to make a stiff batter. Add the egg. Beat well with a wooden spoon for three minutes or so. [*If you wish to use your electric mixer, low speed, add only a cup of the flour, and then beat in the remainder by hand.*] Cover the bowl and let batter rise in a warm place (80° to 85°F) until doubled in bulk. This will take from 40 to 60 minutes. Stir down and turn into a well-greased casserole dish with about a quart-and-a-half capacity.

If you use smaller casseroles, or even individual-sized soufflé dishes, be sure that the diameter of the top is equal to or greater than the bottom. Don't try using a bean pot: the bread will be trapped inside! Fill smaller casseroles two-thirds full only. Cover dish and let rise for a half-hour. [*Preheat oven to 350°F.*] Bake for 40 to 50 minutes, or until done. Loosely cover the loaf with aluminum foil to prevent excessive browning the last 15 minutes. Turn out to cool on a rack.

*Notes:*_____

_____

_____

_____

_____

_____

*Date first tried:*_____

∾ Mincemeat Bread ∾

This casserole bread is made by the mother of a family who claim they don't really like mincemeat pies. They have no complaints about this bread, however! Recipe contributed by Grace McFarland, New York

Yields: One or two loaves, depending on your casserole

1+ cup mincemeat (8 or 9 oz., depending on packaging)
½ cup water
2 cups all-purpose flour
1 cup whole wheat flour
2 teaspoons baking powder
1 teaspoon baking soda
1 teaspoon salt
¼ teaspoon powdered ginger (optional)

1 lemon rind, grated
½ cup cold cooked rice
⅓ cup unsulphered molasses
1¾ cups sweet milk
1 egg, lightly beaten
½ cup pecans, chopped or broken (optional), dusted with flour

 One well-greased casserole or soufflé dish, 2-quart capacity

In a saucepan, break up into small pieces the packaged mincemeat (if you are using the kind which comes in jars it is much moister, and you will need less water). Pour the water over it. Cook over a low-medium heat, stirring constantly, until all the lumps are dissolved. Now boil until mixture is almost dry—this takes just a couple of minutes or so, so *do not leave the stove.* Let the mixture cool in a good-sized mixing bowl. Combine the flours with the baking powder, soda, salt, ginger and grated lemon rind. Stir the dry ingredients into the cooled mincemeat. Mix the rice, molasses, milk and egg and stir into batter. Stir the nutmeats and a tablespoon of flour together, then fold into the batter. The flour keeps the nuts from sinking in the early stage of baking. [*Preheat oven to 350°F.*] Pour batter into greased casserole and let sit for 10 minutes while oven heats. Bake for 45 to 60 minutes, or until done. Cover loosely with foil after a half-hour if the bread seems to be browning too quickly.

THE WONDERFUL LITTLE GIANT MEAT CUTTER.

Notes: _____
_____
_____
_____
_____
_____
_____
_____

Date first tried: _____

⇜ Spider Cornbread ⇝

Spiders are the cast iron skillets with three little legs and a long handle that were used for cooking over the coals in the fireplace. By using a long-legged trivet and a lid for the skillet, you can try baking this cornbread the 18th century way in your fireplace, over raked coals. But you can certainly make this fabulous old-fashioned "custard" cornbread in a heavy iron skillet or other heavy baking pan and bake it in an oven.

Notes: _____

_____

_____

_____

_____

_____

_____

Date first tried: _____

Yields: One 9" loaf

1⅓ cup cornmeal,
   stone-ground white
⅓ cup all-purpose flour
1 teaspoon baking soda
2 teaspoons sugar
½ teaspoon salt

2 cups sweet milk
1 cup buttermilk or
   sour milk
2 eggs, well-beaten
2 tablespoons butter or
   strained bacon fat

 One 9" iron skillet or heavy 9" square baking dish

[*Preheat oven to 350°F.*] In a good-sized mixing bowl, combine the cornmeal, flour, baking soda, sugar and salt. Beat in a cup each of the sweet milk and buttermilk, plus the eggs. Meanwhile heat skillet in oven and when it is hot, take it out and melt the fat or butter in it, turning the pan to coat the entire bottom and sides with fat. Pour the batter in the skillet. Carefully pour the second cup of sweet milk over the batter, but *do not stir.* This is what makes the custard layer. Bake 35 to 50 minutes until done. It will be golden brown and springy to the touch. Cool a bit and cut in wedges or squares and serve with butter.

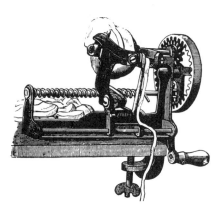

Notes:_____

_____

_____

_____

_____

_____

_____

_____

Date first tried:_____

❧ Apple Cornbread ❧

This is a quick and easy cornbread, with a surprising texture. If you have your own apple trees, or crabapple trees, this recipe gives you one more way to use your apples. For a nice simple dessert, stir the chopped apples in a mixture of two tablespoons of molasses or brown sugar, a tablespoon of lemon juice and a half teaspoon of ground ginger. Recipe by June Folsom, New Hampshire

Yields: One 8″ panful

1 cup all-purpose flour
1 cup cornmeal, white or
   yellow
1 tablespoon sugar
1 teaspoon salt
4 teaspoons baking powder
1 egg, lightly beaten

1 cup sweet milk
3 tablespoons melted shortening (butter, margarine
   or bacon fat)
¾ to 1 cup apples, peeled and
   finely chopped

 One well-greased baking pan, 8″ x 8″ x 2″

[*Preheat oven to 400°F.*] In a good-sized mixing bowl, sift the flour, cornmeal, sugar, salt and baking powder together. Stir in a mixture of the egg and milk, and then add melted shortening. Stir in the apple pieces (don't cut them too tiny), just enough to distribute throughout the batter. Spoon batter into greased pan and bake for about 20 minutes until done, golden brown and springy to the touch. Cut into chunks to serve—hot or warm.

⮌ Colonel Kernel Bread ⮌

Haven't you always wanted to call someone, or something, "Colonel Kernel"? I hope so. If not, you can call this cornbread anything you like except no good!

Yields: One 9″ panful

1 cup whole kernel corn, canned and drained, or freshly-scraped off the cob

2 tablespoons butter or strained bacon fat

1¼ cup cornmeal, yellow

¾ cup all-purpose flour

2 teaspoons baking powder

1 teaspoon baking soda

1 teaspoon salt

2 eggs, lightly beaten

1 tablespoon shortening, melted

1 cup buttermilk (sweet milk is fine too)

 One lightly greased pan, 9″ x 9″ x 2″

Sauté a cup of whole corn (well-drained if you use canned corn) in butter or bacon fat, stirring constantly, until lightly browned and sweet-smelling. [*Preheat oven to 425°F.*] Sift dry ingredients into a good-sized mixing bowl and stir in the eggs, one more tablespoon of melted shortening, and the buttermilk. Now stir in the browned corn kernels, without draining the fat from them. Spoon into greased pan and bake for about 25 minutes, or until done. Serve hot.

VARIATION: If you use a 9″ cast iron skillet to sauté the corn, you may use the same skillet for baking. Turn corn out, when browned, into the batter, and before pouring batter back into the pan, lightly wipe it out. OR, grease two muffin pans (to make about 14 2″ muffins) and fill each cup two-thirds full. Bake muffins for about 20 to 25 minutes, until done.

Notes: _____
_____
_____
_____
_____
_____
_____
_____

Date first tried: _____

≈ Jalapeño Cornbread ≈

This bread is fabulous with chili (meatless, beanless or anyway you fix it), or with rich, thick tomato, bean and hotdog soup. Fill out the menu with spinach salad, crisp dill pickles and something cold to drink. Recipe contributed by Mario Montrose, New Mexico

Yields: One 9″ panful

2 cups cornmeal, preferably
   yellow
½ cup all-purpose flour
1 tablespoon baking powder
1 teaspoon salt
2 eggs, well-beaten
3 tablespoons oil
1 cup sweet milk
½ to 1 cup cooked rice
   (whatever's left over)
1 cup sharp Cheddar cheese,
   grated
1 small onion, grated (or 2
   tablespoons minced
   instant onion)
⅓ cup canned Jalapeño chili
   peppers, drained and chopped
paprika

 One greased baking pan, 9″ square

[*Preheat oven to 375°F.*] In a large mixing bowl, stir the first four dry ingredients together. In a small bowl, beat the eggs, stir in the oil and milk, and mix into the flour/meal mixture. Stir in the cooled cooked rice (a great use for leftover rice), cheese, onion and chopped peppers. Take care while chopping the Jalapeños—the juice will burn your eyes if splashed or rubbed into them. You may want to remove many of the seeds too, as you chop, because they are exceedingly hot. Spoon batter into greased pan, spread evenly with a rubber spatula, and dust with paprika. Bake for about 30 minutes, or until done. Cut into squares. Serve hot, warm or cold—your choice.

Notes:_____

_____

_____

_____

_____

_____

_____

Date first tried:_____

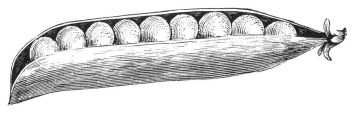

∽ Pease Porridge Cornbread ∾

"Pease Porridge hot, pease porridge cold" —This cornbread won't have time to get old! This is a very pretty cornbread with a great flavor. Pass me some more, please.
LCF

Yields: One panful

1 cup cornmeal, yellow
¾ cup all-purpose flour
2 teaspoons baking powder
1 teaspoon salt
½ cup sweet milk
1 egg, beaten
3 tablespoons oil or melted
   shortening

½ cup sweet milk
1 cup green peas, puréed

½ teaspoon crushed rosemary
   leaves
1 teaspoon salt
2 tablespoons sugar
1 egg, lightly beaten
2 teaspoons baking powder
1 cup cornmeal, white or
   yellow
1 tablespoon oil or melted
   shortening
½ cup sweet milk

 One very well-greased pan, 8″ x 8″ x 2″ or 9″ iron skillet

This takes two good-sized mixing bowls. In the first one, mix the dry ingredients from the list above left—cornmeal, flour, baking powder—and stir in the egg, milk and oil. Then, in a blender, pour a half cup of milk and the crushed rosemary leaves and a cup of green peas and purée. Use fresh or thawed frozen peas. Personally I don't like canned peas, but if you do, you might try them—well drained. [*Preheat oven to 350°F.*] Put pea purée into second mixing bowl and stir in the rest of the ingredients from list above right. Into a well-greased shallow baking pan or dish, spoon the yellow cornmeal mixture, and spread out evenly. Pour on, and evenly spread the pea mixture. Carefully pour a half cup of milk over the top and *do not stir*. Bake for 25 to 35 minutes, or until done. Serve hot.

Notes: _____
_____
_____
_____
_____
_____
_____
_____

Date first tried: _____

❧ Corn Pones ❧

We sometimes call cornmeal "Indian meal," because it was the Indians of the Americas who first recognized corn, or maize, as a foodstuff. They also cultivated it, and the many hybrids today are the result. The word "pone" is also probably from the Indian oppone, *the word for a kind of baked bread. It is possibly no coincidence, because studies have shown how interrelated many of the world's ancient languages are, that* panis *is Latin for bread, and of course* pain *is French for bread. We bake pones in the oven now, but they were once cooked in front of a hot fire or in the ashes near raked coals in a fireplace. Wood ashes, which are a crude carbonate, had to be dusted off the pones, but whatever clung to them made them, in the words of one 19th century writer, "an excellent food for dyspeptics."*

Yields: About a dozen pones

2½ cups cornmeal, white or
    yellow
1 cup boiling water
1 teaspoon salt

2 tablespoons shortening
    (lard or bacon fat preferred)
½ cup buttermilk
1 egg, well-beaten
1 teaspoon baking soda

 One well-greased baking sheet

[*Preheat oven to 375°F.*] Combine cornmeal, water, salt and shortening in a mixing bowl. Mix thoroughly. Stir in the buttermilk, egg and soda to make a stiff batter. Spoon out oval pones, shaping them like goose eggs with a greased spoon, onto greased baking sheet. Bake for about 30 minutes until pones are done and crisp on outside. Serve hot.

*Notes:*_____
_____
_____
_____
_____
_____
_____
_____

*Date first tried:*_____

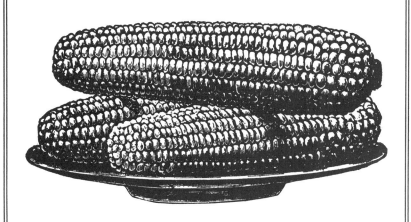

∾ Fried Hoecakes ∾

These are the simplest of the oldtime cornbreads. Supposedly they were first baked during the 18th century by slaves, slapped onto the broad angled blades of cotton-field hoes, and baked in front of a fire. This seems hard to believe, although by removing the handle of the hoe it just might work. Perhaps, in the spirit of "journey cakes," hoecakes were taken to the fields to eat while hoeing. The recipe here calls for frying in a skillet.

Yields: Four to 6 cakes

1 cup boiling water
2 cups cornmeal, white or yellow
1 teaspoon salt
3 tablespoons lard or bacon fat
1 teaspoon baking powder
½ cup shortening

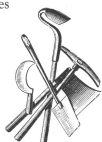

 One cast iron skillet, 12″

Boil about a cup of water, and stir enough of it into a mixing bowl of cornmeal, salt, fat and baking powder to make a moist dough which can be shaped with wet hands into cakes. (Many people make it without baking powder. Originally, if any leavening was used at all, it was probably a crude baking powder called salaeratus, made from potash—sifted wood ashes.) Heat enough shortening in the skillet to make it about a quarter inch deep. Over medium-low to medium heat (you know your stove best) cook the cakes about 15 minutes and then turn over to brown the other side. Serve hot with corn syrup, molasses or honey.

Notes: _____
_____
_____
_____
_____
_____
_____
_____

Date first tried: _____

⌘ Hush Puppies ⌘

These fritters are served with catfish throughout the South. They are supposed to have originated in Florida, where canal fishermen would stir up a batch to cook with their catch. To shush the dogs, whining for handouts of fish, the fishermen would toss them pieces of cornmeal fritter.

Yields: Hush puppies for six to eight people or two hungry dogs

2 cups fine white cornmeal
2 teaspoons baking powder
1 teaspoon salt
2 dashes cayenne pepper
1 large onion, minced
1 egg
1 cup buttermilk
½ cup water
fat for frying

 One cast iron skillet, 12″ is best

Have your skillet hot, and add enough fat for deep frying. Heat fat to about 370°F. Cook half your fish and half the puppies in the fat at the same time. In a good-sized mixing bowl, combine the dry ingredients. Mix the onion, egg, milk and water and stir into the cornmeal. If necessary, add more cornmeal to make a stiff batter. Carefully drop, so you don't splatter yourself, large spoonsful of batter into the fat. Drain fish and hush puppies and serve hot.

Notes:_____

_____

_____

_____

_____

_____

_____

Date first tried:_____

HUSH PUPPIES

Hound puppies howls in Georgia
Hound puppies howls at home
I 'spect dey cries in Paris
An' I her'd dey squeks in Rome
But de hunters an' de hounds
Dey don't make a sound
After you all passes
Dese here pones around
You chops a cup of onions
An' you chops em' mighty fine
'Ca'se de hunters an' de hounds
Dey all is here to dine
But make dis corn-cake batter
An' dey'll make dem plates to shine
A cup of flour, three cups of meal
All de eggs dat you can steal
Four little spoons of baking powder
An' one o' common salt
A cup o' milk, you fries 'em then
An' no man cries a halt.

A poem by Hannah K. Wright, Wilmington, North Carolina. First appeared in Favorite Recipes of The Lower Cape Fear, © *The Ministering Circle, Wilmington, 1955*

Jonakins

I'll hedge my bet on the correct name for these fried corn cakes by using a name which dates back at least to the 17th century. Jonakins (spelled jonikins two centuries later) are what people argue are called "journey cakes," "johnny cakes" or—in Rhode Island—"jonnycakes." It was and is a perfect traveller's food, but I leave it up to you which name you prefer.

Yields: About 14 to 16 small cakes

1 cup cornmeal, water-ground white is best
1 teaspoon salt
1 cup boiling water
Scant ½ cup sweet milk
1 teaspoon sugar (optional), or
2 tablespoons molasses (optional)

 One greased griddle or heavy frying pan

Put cornmeal and salt in a ceramic or plastic mixing bowl and pour in the boiling water to scald it. Give the meal time to absorb the water and swell. Beat in the milk gradually until you have a batter just a bit slower-pouring than pancake batter. Add the sugar or molasses if you like. Heat the skillet or griddle and grease well. Spoon the jonakins on the griddle and cook about eight to 10 minutes before turning to brown the other side. Serve hot, with butter and syrup, or pack as part of a snack for a car or train trip!

NEW HOUSEHOLD

WHITE, WARNER & CO.
MANUFACTURERS OF STOVES, RANGES &c.
TAUNTON, MASS.

Notes: _____

_____

_____

_____

_____

_____

_____

_____

Date first tried: _____

JOHNNY-CAKE

Sift one quart of Indian meal into a pan; make a hole in the middle, and pour in a pint of warm water, adding one teaspoonful of salt; with a spoon mix the meal and water gradually into a soft dough; stir it very briskly for a quarter of an hour or more, till it becomes light and spongy; then spread the dough smooth and evenly on a straight, flat board (a piece of the head of a flour-barrel will serve for this purpose); place the board nearly upright before an open fire, and put an iron against the back to support it; bake it well; when done, cut it in squares; send it hot to table, split and buttered.

From the Universal Cookery Book, *edited by Gertrude Strohm, 1887*

⇜ 1-2-3 Spoon Bread ⇝

This is very much like spider cake (page 45), in that it is a custardy cornbread. But it is served softer—dished out with a spoon—and it is meant to be a starchy "vegetable," in place of mashed potatoes or rice, rather than a bread. It may be sheer perversity, but I love it cold, with molasses and milk.

Yields: One casserole-full, enough for six or eight people

1 cup cornmeal, white stone-ground is best
2 cups sweet milk (or 1 buttermilk, 1 sweet), scalded
3 tablespoons butter or margarine
1 teaspoon salt
2 teaspoons sugar
3 eggs

 One well-greased casserole, 2-quart capacity

The best way to get a creamy pudding-like spoon bread is to scald the cornmeal before baking. Put the cornmeal in a good-sized ceramic mixing bowl and pour in the scalding hot milk, stirring constantly. Stir in butter, salt and sugar. Let the meal absorb the milk and cool for about 10 minutes. [*Preheat oven to 350°F.*] Beat in eggs until the batter is creamy and thoroughly blended. Pour batter into well-greased casserole and bake for about 40 minutes or until lightly crisped at the sides and top, but not quite as firmly springy to the touch as cornbread. Serve hot with butter or gravy.

NOTE: You can keep the top moist by pouring a few spoonsful of sweet milk over the top during baking. Do this two or three times. Baking time must be increased by about 15 to 20 minutes.

Notes: _____

_____

_____

_____

_____

_____

_____

_____

Date first tried: _____

Notes:_____

_____

_____

_____

_____

_____

_____

Date first tried:_____

ASK FOR
THE NEW KIND
SALTED PEANUTS

∽ Goober Spoon Bread ∽

The word goober *is probably an adaptation of* nguba, *a West African word for peanut. This tasty spoon bread has a very delicate peanut flavor, a real Southern treat to serve with roast pork or turkey.*

Yields: One panful, enough for six to eight people

½ cup hominy grits

½ cup cornmeal, white stoneground is best

1 cup water

3 tablespoon smooth peanut butter

1 cup buttermilk (or sour milk)

½ teaspoon salt

½ teaspoon baking soda

3 eggs, well-beaten

 One well-greased casserole, 2-quart capacity

Put grits, cornmeal and the water in a saucepan and cook over a medium heat for about five or six minutes, stirring constantly to make sure the mixture doesn't lump up or stick to the pan bottom. Add a little water if necessary. [*Preheat oven to 350°F.*] Remove saucepan from heat and beat in peanut butter, milk, salt and soda. Let cool enough to add eggs and beat them in quickly. Turn batter into well-greased dish and bake for about 25 to 30 minutes, until done. It should be moist inside and light brown and a bit crusty on top. Serve hot, and spoon out directly onto plates.

❧ Rice Spoon Bread ❧

Just because it makes a really different texture, I like to make this recipe with a half cup of Rice Crispies.® If you don't have any, reduce the liquid by about ⅛ cup. This spoon bread is also good, to my mind and stomach, cold with syrup and milk. I've never tried it, but I think some time I'll make it with currants or raisins—a variety of rice pudding.

Notes: _____
_____
_____
_____
_____
_____
_____
_____

Date first tried:_____

Yields: One panful

3 eggs, lightly beaten

1½ cups cooked rice

1 cup cornmeal, white
   stone-ground is best

2 cups sweet milk

2 tablespoons melted
   shortening or butter

2 teaspoons baking powder

2 teaspoons salt

2 teaspoons sugar

½ cup Rice Crispies®

 One greased casserole or baking dish, 2-quart capacity [*Preheat oven to 350°F.*] In a large mixing bowl, beat three eggs lightly. Mix in the cooked rice, cornmeal, milk, melted shortening, baking powder, salt and sugar. Beat well, then fold in the Rice Crispies®. Pour batter into a greased dish and bake about 45 to 60 minutes until done. Serve hot with roast pork, meatloaf or seafood.

VARIATION: Leave out sugar and fold in ½ cup grated sharp Cheddar. Bake as above.

*Notes:*_____

_____

_____

_____

_____

_____

_____

*Date first tried:*_____

∽Mammam's Boston Brown Bread∾

This famous steamed bread is slow-cooking, and it fills the kitchen with a marvelous smell. Old cookbooks call for everything from lard pails and coffee cans to melon molds. Whatever you use, do not fill more than a scant two-thirds full, and have some kind of cover which will fit securely or can be tied on with string. My mother's mother used to make some loaves in half-pound baking powder cans, very good as gifts. This isn't Mammam's recipe, but I've called it after her anyway.

Yields: About three one-pound loaves

1 cup rye flour
1 cup cornmeal, yellow
1 cup whole wheat flour
2 teaspoons baking soda
1 teaspoon baking powder
1 teaspoon salt

¾ cup molasses
1½ cups buttermilk (or
  sour milk)
1 cup raisins (optional),
  dusted with flour

 Three well-greased coffee cans, pudding molds, or other cylindrical cans with a 1-quart capacity. Grease lids too. You also need a large kettle or ham boiler.

Sift the dry ingredients together in a big mixing bowl. Stir in molasses and milk. Stir in floured raisins, if desired. Put greased wax paper discs in the bottom of each well-greased can or mold —this will make it easier to shake out your loaves. Pour batter into cans so that they are slightly less than ⅔ full. Make "lids" of doubleweight aluminum foil, well-greased on the inside. Fold them over can tops and tie in place, tightly, with string. Do not use plastic coffee can lids. Put a rack in the kettle, place the cans on it and fill with enough hot water to come halfway up around the cans. Put cover on kettle and turn heat to medium or medium-high. You want the water to boil *slowly* for about two hours, or more, and it may be necessary to add more hot water occasionally during the steaming process. [*Preheat oven to 300°F.*]

   At two hours you may want to test the progress of your bread by removing a can from the kettle, taking off the lid and touching top to see if it is springy and moist but not sticky. The bread should have risen to the top of the can or mold. If it seems ready, remove all the cans, take off the lids and bake in the oven for about 15 to 20 minutes. Let cool in the cans for 10 minutes before turning out on a rack. If you have trouble, slip knife around inside can to loosen.

Steamed Indian Bread

This is a simple variety of steamed bread, undoubtedly first made by the Indians with nothing but corn, water, and perhaps some kind of sweetener.

Yields: One loaf

2 cups cornmeal, white or yellow
1 cup whole wheat flour
1 teaspoon salt
1 teaspoon baking soda
¾ cup molasses
2 cups milk

 One well-greased can, for example a 1-pound coffee can

Mix the dry ingredients in a good-sized bowl. Beat in the molasses and milk—vigorously for two minutes. Grease a coffee can (or other 1-quart mold) as directed for Boston Brown Bread, including the greased wax paper bottom and foil lid. Fill ⅔ full and place on a rack in a covered kettle. Pour boiling water around mold, extending halfway up the can. Cover and steam for about two hours, over medium to medium-high heat, until done. Replenish water when necessary. Serve sliced, hot and buttered.

Notes: _____

_____

_____

_____

_____

_____

_____

*Date first tried:*_____

≈ Whopovers ≈

There are almost as many possible good-natured arguments about how to make pop-overs (or what to call them) as there are about cornbreads. The biggest difference be-tween popover recipes has to do with using a hot oven or cold oven and hot pans or cold pans. Next in importance is the question about beating the eggs: creamy froth or simply blended? Finally, what do you call them? Popovers, breakfast puffs (as in colonial Williamsburg) or puff popps (as in the deeper South)? The recipe on this page is hot oven/hot pan/creamy eggs. And you can see what I decided to call them!

Yields: About nine to 12 popovers

1 cup all-purpose flour	1 cup sweet milk
¼ teaspoon salt	2 eggs, well-beaten and thick
1 tablespoon melted butter	

Pre-heated then well-greased iron muffin pans or thick custard cups —enough for 12 popovers. Use a pan with nine cups, plus three custard cups, if necessary. Popover pans, because the cups are deeper than they are wide, are best by far: the whole idea of these hollow muffins is height.

[*Preheat oven to 400°F.*] This recipe shouldn't take more than five minutes from start to oven, so you may want to put your pans and/or cups in the oven to heat while you mix up the in-gredients. Remember that as soon as the batter is ready, you will quickly have to grease the cups and pans, pour in the bat-ter, and get it all into the oven in record time. Otherwise you aren't giving the hot oven method its chance!

Sift flour in a bowl with the salt and sugar. Stir in half the milk and all the butter and beat until smooth, then beat in the rest of the milk. With an eggbeater or a handmixer, beat the eggs until they are creamy and lemon-colored. Add to the rest of the batter and beat two minutes with eggbeater or one minute with electric handmixer. Take pans or cups (set on a baking sheet) from the oven, grease quickly with a piece of heavily buttered paper towel, and pour each cup just over half full of batter. If the batter hisses as it goes into the cups, great!

Bake in oven for about 30 minutes, *without opening the oven door.* After a half hour, open door, turn oven off, open tops of the popovers with the point of a paring knife—just a slit to let the steam escape, and let them sit in the closed oven another five minutes. This may or may not keep them from collapsing. Serve hot with butter and jam.

VARIATIONS: Leave out sugar and add a half-cup of grated hard cheese and a little dash of cayenne pepper to batter; or add a heap-ing teaspoon of dried sweet herbs to flour before making batter.

*Notes:*_____

_____

_____

_____

_____

_____

_____

*Date first tried:*_____

∼ Craig's Sister's Popovers ∼

Once upon a time, Barbara brought a simple popover recipe home from a Brownie troop meeting. Her little brother made the recipe first, and it became known in the family as Craig's popover recipe. "Craig, why don't you make those wonderful popovers for us!" With this book, credit is being restored where credit is due. This is a cold oven, cold pan, lightly-beaten-egg recipe. It works and it is good. Recipe contributed by Barbara Tomkinson Reich and Craig Tomkinson, Florida and Connecticut

Yields: Nine popovers

1 cup milk
1 cup all-purpose flour
1 teaspoon salt
1 tablespoon sugar
2 eggs

 Greased muffin pans, cast iron popover pans or ceramic custard cups.

Mix the flour, milk, sugar and salt in a blender very thoroughly. Add the eggs but don't overbeat, just blend. Fill greased muffin cups about ⅔ full. Put in cold oven and turn heat to 425°F. Bake for about 30 minutes until popped over and golden brown. When removed from the cups they may or may not stay puffed up, but they taste wonderful either way. Serve hot, buttered and enlivened with honey, jam or preserves.

FADGES

This recipe is quoted in its entirety from an 1896 copy of The Original Boston Cooking-School Cook Book *by Fannie Farmer.*

1 cup entire wheat flour.
1 cup cold water.

Add water gradually to flour, and beat with Dover egg-beater until very light. Bake as Pop-overs.

Notes: _____
_____
_____
_____
_____
_____
_____
_____

Date first tried: _____

≈ Standard Muffins ≈

This first recipe for muffins is a very basic one—it could be the recipe that you adapt and experiment with to create your family's favorites. Muffins are easier-than-pie to make, and supposedly the only rule is: do not overmix. Beating the batter causes the gluten in wheat flour to develop and this toughens the muffins. Muffins are supposed to be soft—in fact, the word comes from the Old French moufflet, *meaning soft bread.*

Yields: Twelve medium-sized muffins

2 cups all-purpose flour

3 teaspoons baking powder

½ teaspoon salt

2 tablespoons sugar

1 egg, well-beaten

1 cup milk

¼ cup melted shortening,
   preferably butter

 Greased muffin pan(s) with 12 cups

[*Preheat oven to 400°F.*] If you are using heavy cast iron muffin pans, preheat them too, ungreased. In a large mixing bowl, combine the flour, baking powder, salt and sugar. Mix egg and milk and *stir*, don't beat, into flour. Stir in melted butter and heed not the lumps! Spoon into greased (and perhaps pre-heated) muffin pan, filling each cup two-thirds full. Bake about 20 minutes until golden brown. Serve hot. If you plan to serve later, turn out to cool on a rack and then reheat before serving.

Notes: _____

_____

_____

_____

_____

_____

_____

_____

Date first tried: _____

◇ Bran Muffins ◇

Bran muffins are a version of the old-fashioned "Graham gems." Those were made with coarse whole wheat flour that had the bran left in, according to the dictates of Dr. Sylvester Graham, a 19th-century reverend who was way ahead of his time on the subject of healthful eating. These bran muffins are very tasty—"earthy and good," as Fanny Farmer called hers.

Yields: Twelve medium-sized muffins

1 cup bran
1 cup sweet milk
1 egg, slightly beaten
2 tablespoons melted butter or margarine
1 cup all-purpose flour
3 teaspoons baking powder
½ teaspoon salt
⅓ cup unsulphered molasses
½ cup raisins, chopped prunes or dates (all optional)

 Muffin pan(s) with 12 cups

[*Preheat oven to 400°F.*] Prepare muffin pan(s) as for Standard Muffins—that is, heat the heavy ones before greasing, or simply grease lightweight ones. Combine bran, milk, egg and butter in a mixing bowl and let soak for 10 minutes. Stir in flour, baking powder, salt, molasses and raisins, if desired. Don't beat, and do not stir longer than it takes to dampen the flour. Spoon into pan, filling cups about two-thirds full. Bake about 20 to 25 minutes until done. A broomstraw stuck in the center should come out dry.

VARIATION: Use muffin rings (or small-sized tuna fish cans, lids and bottoms removed, and well-washed) set on a hot buttered griddle or frying pan. Fill each ring half full of batter, and cook until risen and brown. Turn muffins and rings over and cook another couple of minutes before serving.

Notes: *Very good*

Date first tried: *10-24-82*

∾ Corn Muffins ∾

Most of the cornbread recipes can also be used for making muffins—although the custardy ones have to be dehydrated by taking out a cup of milk. The following recipe is good for muffins or for cob-shaped cornsticks. If you are interested in antique kitchen collectibles, and in making muffins, look for various fancy cast iron muffin pans.

Yields: About 12 muffins

1½ cups cornmeal, white or yellow
½ cup all-purpose flour
2 tablespoons sugar
2 teaspoons baking powder
½ teaspoon salt
1 egg, lightly beaten
1 cup sweet milk
3 tablespoons melted shortening

 One greased muffin pan with 12 cups

[*Preheat oven to 400°F.*] In a mixing bowl, combine dry ingredients. Mix milk, egg and shortening, and stir into the dry mixture —just enough to dampen everything. Spoon into greased muffin pans, filling them only two-thirds full, and bake for about 20 to 25 minutes, until done. Serve hot.

VARIATIONS: Use bacon fat instead of shortening; stir in a half cup of crumpled bacon; try a dash of cayenne pepper and some chopped onions.

Notes: _____
_____
_____
_____
_____
_____
_____
_____

Date first tried: _____

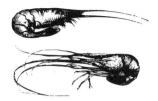

DADDY'S MUFFINS

The recipes on these two pages come from the fertile mind of my father, who is a self-styled muffineer. The banana-carrot muffins were invented just for this book. The batch I ate were sent U.P.S. door-to-door, and a day on the highway didn't take anything away from them. Shrimp muffins are now an old favorite of the family, invented about 1975. Occasionally an experimental recipe doesn't work, or fails the five-mouth taste test: we then credit Daddy's alter ego, Debert, with those muffins. "Debert" was adopted from a misspelled address slip on a piece of junk mail, and we think it has just the right sound for a scapegoat! Recipes by Robert D. Franklin, Virginia

Curried Shrimp Muffins

This is a Far Eastern meal-in-a-muffin. It can be made with chopped frozen or fresh shrimp, canned shrimp, or —best of all, I think —tiny dried shrimp cooked briefly in a pressure cooker. The dried shrimp are available in Oriental food stores.

Notes:_____

_____

_____

_____

_____

_____

Date first tried:_____

Yields: About 24 small muffins

2 cups cooked rice,
   moist and cooled
1 cup shrimp, chopped
1½ teaspoon curry powder
2 eggs, lightly beaten
3 tablespoons cooking oil

 Greased muffin pans for 24 small muffins

[*Preheat oven to 350°F.*] In a mixing bowl, stir the shrimp into the moist cooked rice. Beat the curry powder with the eggs and add the oil. Stir this into the rice and shrimp. Fill greased muffin pans level (these muffins won't rise at all, no matter what). Bake about 20 to 25 minutes until done. The curry powder makes them golden and the baking makes them brown. Serve hot.

≈ Banana-Carrot Muffins ≈

Yields: About 48 to 60 muffins, depending on size

2 cups quick-cooking oatmeal
2 cups all-purpose flour

1½ cup bran
½ cup dry powdered milk
1 teaspoon powdered cinnamon
1 teaspoon salt
4 teaspoons baking powder
4 large ripe bananas, mashed
4 large carrots, grated
2 eggs
½ cup honey
⅓ cup cooking oil
1½ cup sweet milk
1 cup pecans or walnuts,
    chopped or broken

 Lightly greased muffin pans, enough to make
48 muffins, with another pan ready to go if needed

[*Preheat oven to 350°F.*] Combine all the dry ingredients in a large mixing bowl. In another bowl, mash the bananas to nearly liquid consistency. Grate four large or six small carrots into the bananas and mix. Stir in eggs, honey, cooking oil and half the milk. Now add wet ingredients to the dry, adding as much more milk as needed for a batter that "will fall very slowly from a spoon" into the muffin pans. One and a half cups of milk in all is usually sufficient—the size and ripeness of *your* large bananas, and the size of the eggs are factors which determine how much liquid is needed. Stir in the nutmeats if desired. We've grown to crave at least some of Daddy's muffins in a supposedly unorthodox form: dense, coarse-grained and moist. You can have yours that way too by beating them well. Fill muffin tins a little over two-thirds full. Stick a whole nutmeat down in the center of each muffin, if desired. Bake for 20 to 25 minutes, or until browned and done. Tip up sideways in pans to cool, or turn out onto racks. Do not wrap to store until thoroughly cool or they will steam and be soggy.
VARIATION: "Use the same recipe with more bananas and no carrots, or vice versa. Adjust liquid accordingly. Revise recipe to taste for the next baking."

Notes: _____
_____
_____
_____
_____
_____
_____
_____

Date first tried: _____

⤳ Rose Geranium Muffins ⤳

This is an adaptation of a very old recipe. These sweet muffins are excellent with tea, and identification of the flavor will defy all but the best herbalists!

Yields: About 12 muffins

2 cups all-purpose flour
4 teaspoons baking powder
½ teaspoon salt
1 egg, lightly beaten
¾ cup sweet milk
3 tablespoons melted butter
3 tablespoons rose geranium leaves, chopped fine
1 orange peel, grated
12 sugar cubes
melted butter

 Greased muffin pan for 12 muffins

[*Preheat oven to 375°F.*] Sift the flour, baking powder and salt into a bowl. Lightly stir into the flour, until it is dampened, a mixture of the egg, milk and butter. In a very shallow bowl, chop the rose geranium leaves very fine, mix with the grated orange peel and a squirt of orange juice. Spoon muffin batter into greased muffin cups, filling them no more than two-thirds full. Roll each sugar cube in the herb and orange peel mixture to coat. As if you were planting a flower seed, poke your finger into each muffin top and press a sugar cube into the depression. Brush top of each muffin with melted butter, and bake for about 20 minutes, or until done and lightly browned.

Notes:_____

_____

_____

_____

_____

_____

_____

_____

Date first tried:_____

≈ Blueberry Gems ≈

Gems were made in the 19th century in gem pans —heavy cast iron pans with relatively shallow, oblong cups that had rounded bottoms. Gems were also always made with Graham or whole wheat flour and were something like bran muffins. With jewel-like blueberries, the name takes on a new meaning.

Yields: About 16 large muffins

1 cup all-purpose flour
1 cup whole wheat flour
¼ cup sugar
3 teaspoons baking powder
½ teaspoon salt
2 eggs, lightly beaten
¾ cup sweet milk
1 teaspoon vanilla extract
¼ cup melted butter or
    cooking oil
1 cup blueberries (fresh are
    best)

 Heated and greased cast iron gem pans or muffin pans, for 16 muffins

[*Preheat oven to 375°F.*] Heat pans if you are using cast iron ones. Then, in a large mixing bowl, combine the flours, sugar, baking powder and salt. Mix together the eggs, milk, vanilla and butter, then stir the wet mixture into the dry, stirring as little as possible. Fold in the blueberries until well distributed. Spoon into greased muffin pans, filling about two-thirds full. Bake for 20 to 25 minutes, until done. Serve hot.

Notes: _____

_____

_____

_____

_____

_____

_____

_____

Date first tried: 10/27/82

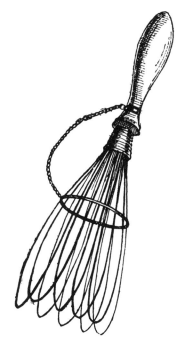

 Oatmeal Muffins

These are plain muffins with nothing but the good taste of oats. If you really want to make them special, use Scotch oatmeal, cooked the long slow way, to bring out the flavor. Have you ever tried dunking muffins? These are great that way. Recipe by John McBurney, Arkansas

Yields: About 12 to 16 muffins

2 eggs, lightly beaten
1 cup cooked oatmeal, cooled
1 cup sweet milk
2 tablespoons melted butter
1½ cup all-purpose flour
2 tablespoons light brown sugar
3 tablespoons baking powder
½ teaspoon salt

Greased muffin pans, for 16 muffins

[*Preheat oven to 400°F.*] Beat eggs in a big mixing bowl and stir in the oatmeal, milk and butter. Mix thoroughly. Sift in the flour, sugar, baking powder and salt and stir well but don't over-mix. Spoon into greased muffin pans, filling each cup two-thirds full. Bake for about 20 to 25 minutes, or until done. Use a broomstraw to test—it should come out dry.

Notes:_____

_____

_____

_____

_____

_____

_____

Date first tried:_____

"EGGS, To Preserve.—Put 12 or more eggs into a small willow-basket and immerse this for 5 seconds in boiling water, containing about 5 lbs. brown sugar per gal.; place the eggs on trays to dry; pack, when cool, small ends down, in an intimate mixture of 1 part of finely powdered charcoal and 2 of dry bran. They will last 6 mos., or more. Scalding water causes the formation of a skin of hard albumen next the inner surface of the shell, and the sugar closes the pores."

From Scammell's Treasure-House of Useful Knowledge, 1881

Notes:_____

_____

_____

_____

_____

_____

_____

Date first tried:_____

∾ Mole Hill Farm Memorial Biscuits ∾
BAKING POWDER

As children, my brother Robbie and I loved the biscuits that my mother made so often for supper. We lived on a farm in Ohio and there were plenty of grandfather apple trees in the side yard. Robbie and I would gather a pan full of the knobby, often worm-bitten apples which old trees produce. Then Mummy would make fresh hot applesauce and fresh hot biscuits, seemingly without effort or fuss, while preparing the rest of the meal. MMMmmm! LCF

Yields: About 20 to 24 biscuits

2 cups all-purpose flour
4 teaspoons baking powder
½ teaspoon salt
⅓ cup shortening
¾ cup sweet milk

 One baking sheet, greased or ungreased

[*Preheat oven to 450°F.*] In a good-sized mixing bowl, sift the flour, baking powder and salt. Cut the shortening in with a pastry blender, fork or crossed knives, or rub it in with the fingers until the pastry resembles coarse crumbs or grains. Add the milk and stir enough to form a ball around a fork. If more milk is needed, add just a tablespoon at a time. Don't let the dough get sticky, and don't beat. Turn out on a flour-dusted surface and knead for 30 seconds or so. Flatten with palms and roll out with rolling pin to half-inch thickness. Dip the biscuit cutter in flour, shake, and cut the biscuits. Don't twist the cutter because it tends to seal the edges and the biscuits aren't as free to rise. If you want crusty biscuits, grease the baking sheet and lay out biscuits an inch apart. If you want soft biscuits, don't grease the sheet, and place the biscuits so they touch. Bake for about 15 minutes, or until light brown. Serve immediately, turned out into a napkin-lined basket.

Old Style Biscuits
BUTTERMILK

Half of what I know about cooking comes either from my mother or Mrs. Burton, who lived for a while at Mole Hill Farm. The following recipe was put on paper for this book, although Mrs. Burton says ". . . most of my cooking I just put together." She puts it together very well, too! Recipe by Willie Lee Burton, Ohio

Yields: About 36 biscuits

3 cups all-purpose flour
2 tablespoons baking powder
1 teaspoon baking soda
½ teaspoon salt
1 pinch of sugar
1 large cook's spoon heaping
   with shortening (pure
   lard is best)
1 cup buttermilk

 Two baking sheets, greased or ungreased

[*Preheat oven to 400°F.*] Put one and a half cups of flour in the sifter. Add the baking powder, baking soda, salt and sugar and sift into a bowl. Add the milk and shortening and mix well with a fork. Then add the rest of the flour and work in real good, so you can roll the dough. Put on floured surface and roll out about half an inch thick. Cut the biscuits out and lay on baking sheets. Grease the sheets if you want a crust, and leave an inch between the biscuits. Or, for soft biscuits, lay them out touching each other on an ungreased sheet. Bake for about 15 minutes, or until done. Serve hot with butter.

_____
_____
_____
_____
_____
_____
_____
_____

*Date first tried:*_____

Christmas Party Beaten Biscuits

"My mother, Margaret Faulkner Mason, married Henry Nichols Faulconer—they were from Kentucky. My maternal grand-father, William Barbour Mason, was quite disturbed when three of his daughters married and moved above the Mason-Dixon Line! The girls had been brought up on all kinds of southern breads, especially beaten biscuits. A box of them was always kept in the pantry with baked Kentucky ham, ready for any emergency, unexpected callers, or snacks. My grand-father gave each one of his daughters a dough kneader when they left home. The kneader is table height with a marble top on a wrought iron stand. At one end there are two steel rollers with a handle to turn them. The rollers are adjustable, and the dough is put through them over and over, with the rollers set closer and closer, until it is the right consistency to cut.

"In 1935, when I inherited the kneader from my mother, I did not know how to make beaten biscuits. I wrote to my aunt for the recipe. I had difficulty at first getting the dough to the proper consistency—it must be stiff and not stick to the roller."
Recipe contributed by Margaret Faulconer Minich, Virginia

Yields: About 34 to 36 biscuits

4 cups all-purpose flour
3 teaspoons sugar
1 teaspoon salt
1 teaspoon baking powder
4 tablespoons chilled lard
1 cup half milk, half ice water

 Two floured but ungreased baking sheets

"Mix dry ingredients together in a large mixing bowl. Cut chilled lard into the dry ingredients (as you would mix pie dough) until it is well crumbled. Add the cold liquid gradually and stir to a stiff dough. Flour the board and the rollers of the kneader lightly. Put dough through rollers until it blisters and is smooth and glossy. [*Preheat oven to 325°F.*] Cut with special beaten biscuit cutter or, if one is not available, cut with a regular biscuit cutter and then prick the tops with a fork. Bake for 20 minutes or until cooked in the center. The biscuits should not brown, and if overcooked become hard. They can be reheated for just a few minutes to serve hot."

NOTE: "I have heard the dough can be beaten with a rolling pin or wooden mallet. Dough must be broken down until it blisters. It takes from 300 to 500 licks to produce blisters." *It is supposed to be possible also to beat with the flat of a hatchet, or to put the dough through a hand-cranked meatgrinder, using the coarse blade.*

Notes:_____
_____
_____
_____
_____
_____
_____

Date first tried:_____

∽ Wheat Germ Drop Biscuits ∾

These flavorful biscuits are considered one of Auntie Rachel's "best inventions" by her family. She creates a new biscuit at least once a month, and can never seem to make enough of them. Recipe contributed by her niece for Rachel Cohen, Illinois

Yields: About 20 biscuits

1½ cups all-purpose flour
3 teaspoons baking powder
½ teaspoon salt
½ teaspoon celery seed
½ cup wheat germ, toasted
⅓ cup shortening
1 egg, well-beaten
⅞ cup sweet milk

 Ungreased baking sheet

[*Preheat oven to 425°F.*] In a large bowl, sift the flour, baking powder, salt and celery seed together to evenly cover bottom of bowl. Sprinkle the wheat germ over the flour. Cut in the shortening with pastry blender or fork until you have a coarse, crumbly mixture. Pour in egg and milk and stir for no longer than a minute. Drop tablespoonsful of dough an inch apart on an ungreased baking sheet. Bake 12 to 15 minutes until light brown.

VARIATION: You may cook these in muffin tins, making larger biscuits by dropping two tablespoons of dough into each lightly greased cup.

Notes: _____
_____
_____
_____
_____
_____
_____
_____

Date first tried:_____

⤲ Spud Biscuits ⤲

Not too surprisingly, this recipe comes from one of the country's potato states. I'm sure that if you live in Maine or on Long Island you are welcome to use this recipe with your local potatoes! Recipe contributed by David Nolty, Idaho

Yields: About 12 biscuits

1 cup mashed potatoes
⅓ cup shortening, melted
1½ cups all-purpose flour
1 teaspoon salt
4 teaspoons baking powder
2 tablespoons honey
½ cup sweet milk

One greased baking sheet

[*Preheat oven to 400°F.*] In a large bowl, mix the mashed potatoes (which you may make from instant potato flakes if you like) and melted shortening. Sift the flour, salt and baking powder into the bowl and stir well. Stir in the honey. Add enough of the milk (you may even need more) to moisten and make a workable soft dough. Turn dough out on a lightly floured surface and knead about 15 times. Pat or roll out to three-fourths of an inch thickness. Cut with floured cutter and place on a greased baking sheet about a half-inch apart. Bake 15 minutes, or until done. Serve hot with butter.

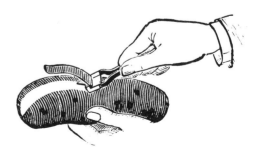

Notes:_____
_____
_____
_____
_____
_____
_____

*Date first tried:*_____

BUY THE CONQUEROR WRINGER.

WARRANTED

BAKING DAY.

DONALDSON BROTHERS, FIVE POINTS, N.Y.

∽ Sweet Potato Biscuits ∽

These are good biscuits to make with leftover baked sweet potatoes —say the day af-
ter Thanksgiving. They are good for little turkey or ham sandwiches, and tasty with
re-heated gravy. Try them split and grilled in a toaster oven with butter, orange mar-
melade and a tiny marshmallow! Recipe contributed by Esther Jean Lee, Georgia

Yields: About 16 biscuits

2 eggs, lightly beaten
1 cup mashed sweet potatoes
2 tablespoons butter or margarine, softened
2 tablespoons molasses or corn syrup
2 cups all-purpose flour
3 teaspoons baking powder
1 teaspoon salt
½ cup sweet milk

 One lightly greased baking sheet

[*Preheat oven to 375°F.*] Beat the eggs lightly in a large mixing
bowl. Combine the mashed sweet potatoes with the eggs and
stir in the softened butter and sweet syrup. Sift in the flour and
baking powder and stir. Add half the milk, stir, then add
enough of the rest of the milk to make a *soft* dough. Turn out
on a lightly floured surface and knead for 30 seconds. Roll out a
half-inch thick and cut the biscuits. Arrange on lightly greased
baking sheet and bake for about 15 to 20 minutes. Serve hot.

Notes: _____
_____
_____
_____
_____
_____
_____
_____

Date first tried: _____

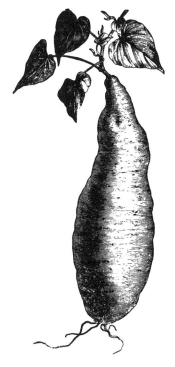

∾ Rosemary Biscuits ∾

These are interesting biscuits and it is fun to cut them with the old-style bridge party cookie cutters in hearts, diamonds, clubs and spades. Rosemary is very distinctive in flavor, and not to everyone's taste, but I think you'll like these.

Yields: About 20 to 24 biscuits

¼ cup hot sweet milk
¼ cup rosemary leaves, finely chopped
2 cups all-purpose flour
3 teaspoons baking powder
½ teaspoon salt
⅓ cup sugar
⅓ cup shortening
¾ cup sweet milk

 Lightly greased baking sheet

Heat the milk close to scalding and stir in the finely chopped rosemary leaves to steep. Let sit until cool. In a good-sized mixing bowl, sift the flour, baking powder, salt and sugar together. Cut in the shortening to form coarse crumbs. Add the rosemary-milk to the flour and stir briefly. Add enough of the remaining milk for the dough to form a ball around the fork. If sticky, sift in just a bit more flour. Turn out and knead about 10 times on a floured surface. Roll lightly to half-inch thickness and cut with floured cutter(s). Arrange on the baking sheet, with about a half-inch between each biscuit and bake about 12 to 15 minutes, until lightly browned. Serve hot or warm.

⤳ Mary Liz's Cheese Biscuits ⤳

Cook these for breakfast or brunch — they smell so delicious that even the fussiest breakfaster will want some. Or make them very small for party hors d'oeuvres; they will be the first things to go. Recipe contributed by Mary Liz Johnson, Virginia

Yields: About 36 biscuits

½ pound butter (2 sticks)
½ pound cheese, grated
2 cups all-purpose flour
1 teaspoon salt
36 pecan halves

 Ungreased baking sheet

[*Preheat oven to 325°F.*] Cream the butter and cheese together in a bowl. Cut in the flour and salt thoroughly. Make small balls, about the size of aggies—those big, old-fashioned marbles—and press a pecan half into the center of each biscuit. Arrange on the baking sheet with about an inch and a half between each biscuit—they will flatten during baking. Bake for about 25 minutes, or until done. Serve after cooling.
VARIATION: Leave out salt. Roll or pat out dough a half-inch thick. Cut biscuits with a floured cutter. Put a scant teaspoon of finely chopped, ready-to-eat prunes on top of half the biscuits. Make a sort of sandwich by placing another unpruned biscuit on top. Do not press together. Bake as above.

Notes: _____
_____
_____
_____
_____
_____
_____
_____

Date first tried: _____

⌐ Dog Biscuits ⌐

This recipe is dedicated to dogs and children. Children can help make these chewy biscuits and form them in any shape they like. The recipe is a rough adaptation of bagels. Veterinarians say that the very best teeth-cleaners for dogs are stale bagels, because they really have to be chewed.

Yields: From 60 to 80 biscuits, depending on size

1 envelope dry yeast
¼ cup warm water
   (105° to 115°F)
1 pinch of sugar
2½ cups whole-wheat flour
½ cup all-purpose flour
½ cup soy flour
½ cup cornmeal
½ cup low-fat milk powder
2 cups cooked egg shells,
   finely crushed

2 eggs, lightly beaten
¼ cup cooking oil
½ cup warm water or vegetable
   broth (105° to 115°F)
½ cup carrots, grated or
½ cup fresh spinach,
   chopped fine
2 garlic cloves, minced or
   pressed

 Large kettle; fry basket to fit; greased baking sheet

Dissolve the yeast in warm water. Add a pinch of sugar to proof. In a large mixing bowl, mix the flours, meal and powdered milk. Take dried shells from two hard boiled eggs and grind in a mortar and pestle to reduce to a fine grit. Stir shells into other dry ingredients. Now stir in the yeast mixture, and the beaten eggs, oil and water. Stir in the grated carrots or minced spinach leaves and stems and the garlic. Beat—if you can—until smooth. Turn out on floured surface and knead for 10 minutes. Put dough in greased bowl, cover, and let double in bulk. This takes an hour. Punch down and divide, by pinching, into as many pieces as desired. The biscuits will rise again, and swell during boiling, so form them smaller than the finished baked biscuit should be. [*Set a kettle, three-fourths full of water, on to boil.*]

Lay formed biscuits (try tiny bagels) on a flour-dusted tray and cover for 25 minutes. When risen, put the fry basket in the kettle and slide small batches of biscuits into the boiling water. Don't crowd too much. Add water when necessary, between batches. Boil five minutes. Remove and drain in colander. [*Preheat oven to 375°F.*] Arrange biscuits on greased baking sheet and bake for 35 minutes or until well-done and brown. Let them get stale and feed two a day.

NOTE: Some humans like these, hot and without the eggshells!

*Notes:*_____

_____

_____

_____

_____

_____

_____

*Date first tried:*_____

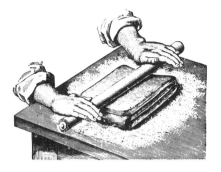

Notes:_____

_____

_____

_____

_____

_____

_____

_____

Date first tried:_____

∽ Parker Home Rolls ∾

Here's an American favorite which this family has adopted as their own. Parker House rolls are a tradition of long standing; they supposedly originated in Boston at the famous Parker House during the mid-19th century, and were simplified versions of the older "pocketbook" rolls. Every American cookbook from then until now has a version. Recipe contributed by The Raymond Parkers, Arkansas

Yields: About 24 to 30 rolls

1 envelope dry yeast
2 tablespoons sugar
¼ cup warm water
  (105° to 115°F)
1½ cup sweet milk, scalded
¼ cup butter (½ stick)

2 eggs, lightly beaten
1 teaspoon salt
4 cups all-purpose flour
1 cup all-purpose flour
  (reserved)
4 tablespoons melted butter

 Greased baking sheets

Dissolve the yeast and sugar in the warm water and proof for five minutes. Heat the milk to scalding, remove from stove, and melt a quarter-cup of butter in it. Let the milk cool a bit, lest it kill the yeast, and combine yeast and milk mixtures in a large mixing bowl. Stir in the eggs. Beat in four cups of flour, mixed with salt, and then as much of the reserve flour as is needed to make a soft dough. Turn out and knead on a floured surface for eight to 10 minutes until smooth and elastic.

Roll the dough around in a greased bowl to coat the surface, cover the bowl with a damp cloth, and put in a warm place (80° to 85°F) to rise and double in bulk. This will take about an hour. Punch down and let rest under the cover for 10 minutes. Turn out again on floured surface and knead for two or three minutes. Divide dough in half and roll out a quarter-inch thick. Cut two-inch rounds with a floured biscuit cutter, and brush the tops with melted butter. Make a ball of the scraps, roll out lightly and cut more rounds. Do not repeat too many times— the rolls will be tough. With the back of a table knife, make a deep crease all the way across each round, slightly off center. Fold the smaller half over the other and press the edges slightly. Place the rolls close together in rows on a greased baking sheet and cover to rise again for 25 minutes. [*Preheat oven to 425°F.*] Bake for about 15 minutes or until light brown and done. Serve immediately or store in the refrigerator and reheat.
NOTE: Use this recipe to create rolls in other shapes, as shown on page 85.

ᐒ Winter Squash Rolls ᐒ

*Americans have a long heritage of making imaginative use of our natural bounties —
pumpkins and other squash, peanuts, corn and sweet potatoes. These rolls are yet
another example of traditional cookery. Make them with any kind of hard-shelled
squash (including pumpkins) or even with sweet potatoes. Some adjustments in
added liquid may be necessary because of varying moisture contents.*

Yields: About 24 rolls

2 envelopes dry yeast
⅓ cup warm water
   (105° to 115°F)
1 pinch sugar
1 cup sweet milk, scalded
4 tablespoons butter,
   margarine or shortening
2 eggs, lightly beaten

2 tablespoons sugar
1 teaspoon salt
½ teaspoon black pepper
¾ cup squash, cooked and
   mashed or sieved
3 cups all-purpose flour
1 cup all-purpose flour
   (reserved)

Notes: _____

_____

_____

_____

_____

_____

_____

Date first tried: _____

 One greased baking sheet

Dissolve the yeast in a third of a cup of water and proof with a
pinch of sugar. Scald a cup of milk, remove from stove, and stir
in the butter or shortening to melt. Set aside to cool for 10 minutes. Combine yeast and milk mixtures. Add the eggs, sugar,
salt, pepper and squash, and stir well. Beat in three cups of flour
and enough of the reserve as needed to make a soft dough (as
opposed to stiff dough). Turn out on a lightly floured surface
and knead gently three or four times. Shape into a ball and roll
around in a buttered bowl to coat. Cover the bowl and put in a
warm spot (80° to 85°F) to rise and double in bulk. This takes
70 to 80 minutes. Punch down and let rise again, covered.

    Divide dough into three or four manageable pieces and roll
each piece out a half-inch thick. Dip a biscuit cutter in flour,
shake, and cut rolls. Take scraps from all cuttings and roll so
that you can cut more, or form "oddballs"—golfball-sized rolls
which will, of course, look quite different from the cut rolls.
These are good ones for the cook or the cook's helpers! Arrange
rolls on a lightly-greased baking sheet, about a half-inch apart.
Cover again and let rest and rise for 30 minutes. [*Preheat oven to
350°F.*] Bake rolls for 25 minutes, or until done. Serve hot and
buttered.

Notes:_____

_____

_____

_____

_____

_____

_____

Date first tried:_____

❧ Maggie's Ice Box Rolls ❧

This old recipe was made for many years by an affectionately-remembered woman named Maggie Davis, who nursed the Rhett children. She became chief cook of the Wrightsville Beach Surf Club when Mrs. Rhett was manager, and her talents became even more widely appreciated. Recipe contributed by Mrs. Haskell S. Rhett, North Carolina

Yields: About 40 plump rolls

2 eggs, lightly beaten
¼ cup sugar
2 teaspoons salt
2 cook's spoons lard
2 cups boiling water
1 yeast cake (or 1 envelope dry yeast)
¼ cup tepid water (105° to 115°F)
6¼ cups all-purpose flour

 Lightly greased baking sheets

In a large mixing bowl, beat the eggs and add the sugar, salt and lard. Pour in the boiling water and stir. Let cool. Dissolve the yeast in tepid water (no higher than 95° for compressed yeast cake) and add to the egg mixture when it has cooled to luke-warm. Beat in enough of the flour to make a smooth soft dough. Knead for eight to 10 minutes and put in a covered bowl. Set to rise in a warm place (80° to 85°F) for an hour. Beat it down again and put in the ice box. Take out and let rise about two hours before baking. Divide, roll out and cut rolls. Bake on lightly greased baking sheets at about 425°F for 15 to 20 minutes, until light brown. Serve hot.

On this page are five ways, among the many which have been invented, to dress up your rolls. Don't do a whole batch in only one design—how much fun it is to hear the "oohs and ahs" of your family and friends when you pass a basket of assorted bowknots, crescents and clover leafs!

CLOVER LEAF

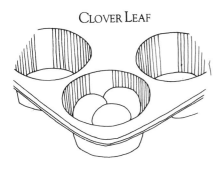

Three small *balls* in each buttered muffin-tin cup

BUTTERHORN

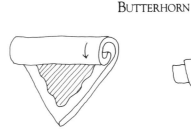

Wedges, rolled ¼″ thick, brushed with butter and rolled up

CRESCENT

Butterhorns that have been curved like a new moon

PARKER HOUSE

Buttered *rounds*, brushed with butter, creased, folded and pinched

BOWKNOT

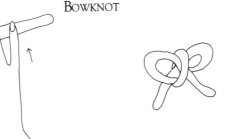

Long rolled *strips* tied loosely in bows

Notes:_____

_____

_____

_____

_____

_____

_____

Date first tried:_____

≈ Cheese Crackers ≈

These crackers are much easier to make than soda crackers and are especially good with spreads and sour cream dips, as well as soups. Everyone but the Walters' parrot likes these for snacking! Recipe by Beulah Walters, Iowa

Yields: About 40 crackers

4 tablespoons butter or shortening
½ cup Cheddar cheese, grated
1 large garlic clove, pressed
2 cups all-purpose flour
½ teaspoon salt
1 teaspoon celery seeds
¼ cup water

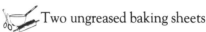 Two ungreased baking sheets

In a large bowl, cream the butter and cheese and mix the pressed garlic in thoroughly. Combine the flour, salt and celery seeds and mix into the cheese mixture. Add enough water to make a rather stiff dough. Knead in the bowl for two or three minutes and form a ball. Pull off pieces and roll between your palms to make small balls—smaller than golf or ping pong balls. [*Preheat oven to 350°F.*] Put balls on *un*greased baking sheets and press flat (a quarter-inch thick) with the bottom of a drinking glass. It is fun to use a pressed glass tumbler that has some design, even though these crackers will not take a sharp impression. After pressing, prick the tops and bake for about 12 to 15 minutes until crisp.

∾ Soda Cracker Digestives ∾

The oldest cracker recipes stress the necessity of kneading or beating the dough as long as possible. One cookbook author of the 19th century even expressed the opinion that ". . . a man has better success than a woman, in making crackers . . ." because he had the stamina required for beating them. These soda crackers (it's the soda which make them "digestives") provide a good time for children, who may beat the dough to their heart's content with impunity. Noise-making of a most constructive sort! Children also enjoy pricking various secret designs and initials in the tops with a #1 knitting needle or cake tester.

Yields: About 50 crackers

4 cups all-purpose flour
1¼ teaspoons baking soda
1 teaspoon salt (optional)
⅓ cup lard or shortening
1 egg, lightly beaten
½ cup sour milk or buttermilk

 Greased baking sheets

In a large bowl, sift the flour, baking soda and salt together. Cut in the lard or shortening with a pastry blender or fork. Mix in the egg, and then add enough of the milk to make a stiff dough. Turn out on a very lightly floured surface and knead for as long as you can stand it. Or beat with a wooden rolling pin or beetle for at least 25 minutes. One old recipe suggests beating with a heavy flat-iron for at least an hour! [*Preheat oven to 400°F.*] Roll out very thin—less than a quarter-inch thick, and cut into squares or rounds with a knife or biscuit cutter. Prick designs in the tops, place on greased baking sheets and bake until tops are lightly browned—12 minutes or so. These can be stored in airtight cracker boxes.

Notes: _____
_____
_____
_____
_____
_____
_____

Date first tried: _____

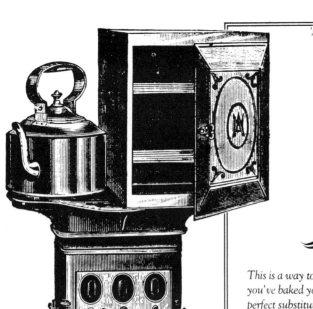

⤙ Sesame Toast Sticks ⤚

This is a way to use a loaf of stale bread, white or whole wheat. You may use bread you've baked yourself, or sliced or unsliced store-bought bread. These are near-perfect substitutes for bread sticks.

Yields: Approximately five sticks per slice

1 loaf stale bread
2 sticks butter or margarine, melted
2 egg whites
2 tablespoons water
⅓ to ½ cup sesame seeds

 Buttered baking sheets

[*Preheat oven to 200°F.*] Trim the crusts from a loaf or partial loaf of bread, after calculating how many sticks you want at five sticks to the slice. Cut slices three-fourths of an inch thick. Cut each slice into strips, about three-quarters of an inch wide. Melt the butter or margarine and brush the tops of the sticks rather generously with butter. Add a quarter teaspoon garlic powder to the butter if you want garlic sticks. Arrange the sticks in rows on a buttered baking sheet. Bake in the slow oven for an hour to 90 minutes, until the sticks are crisp and lightly browned. If they seem to be browning too quickly, lay a piece of aluminum foil over them and reduce the heat slightly. Remove from oven and let cool for five minutes. [*Turn oven up to 350°F.*] Beat the egg whites in two tablespoons of water. Brush the tops of the sticks with egg white and sprinkle with sesame seeds. Pop back in the oven for 10 or 12 minutes to brown. Serve like bread sticks.

*Notes:*_____
_____
_____
_____
_____
_____
_____
_____

*Date first tried:*_____

⤙ Peanut Sticks ⤚

"Peanut sticks are good with coffee, tea, sherry or drinks of any kind. All ages love them, and I have never served them that people did not ask for the recipe. The other day my husband wanted some and the only bread I had was sliced very very thin. I used it and my husband thinks they were the best ever. Wish I had some to send you, but they are all gone!" Recipe by Hannah K. Wright, North Carolina

Yields: About 80 to 100 sticks, depending on bread slices

1 large loaf of sliced bread (not too fresh)
12 ounce jar of smooth peanut butter
½ cup salad oil
cornflake crumbs

 Ungreased baking sheets

[*Preheat oven to 200°F.*] "Cut the bread slices into five or six sticks per slice. I used to cut the crusts off the bread, but don't do it anymore. Arrange sticks on cookie sheets and place in the oven for one to two hours until bread is very crisp. Meanwhile mix the peanut butter and oil in the top of a double boiler. I leave the mixture on the stove at low heat.

"Drop the dried bread sticks, a few at a time, into the melted peanut butter mixture. Use a slotted spoon to take them out. Let drip a little, then toss them in cornflake crumbs until coated. They will keep for weeks in a closed container."

Notes: _____
_____
_____
_____
_____
_____
_____
_____

Date first tried: _____

∽ Fancy Tasting Butter ∾

Breads and butter are perfect complements, and it is up to you whether you prefer sweet or salted butter. Here are some gussied-up butters which taste particularly good either on herb breads (such as Cheryl's Garden Bread on page 12), on plain breads (such as Spud Biscuits on page 76), or on sweet breads (such as Caraway Bread on page 36).

The procedure for all is simple: (1) soften the butter; (2) add the liquid, and/or (3) blend in the flavorings; (4) allow to mellow—but not melt; (5) dish into a small bean pot or little crock; and (6) chill to firm before serving.

SUMMER SAVORY BUTTER

1 stick butter
1 teaspoon savory
1 teaspoon dry mustard

REFRESHING BUTTER

1 stick sweet butter
2 tablespoons lemon juice
¼ cup mint leaves, minced

SPICY BUTTER

1 stick butter
1 medium garlic clove, pressed
1 tablespoon lemon juice
2 dashes Worcestershire sauce

DILLY BUTTER

1 stick butter
1 tablespoon minced fresh
    dillweed, or
1 teaspoon dillseed
1 raw string bean, sliced as
    thin as possible

BASIL BUTTER

1 stick butter
2 teaspoons lemon juice
2 tablespoons fresh basil,
    minced
½ teaspoon black pepper

CINNAMON BUTTER

1 stick butter
1 tablespoon maple syrup
1 teaspoon brown sugar
1 tablespoon sweet milk
½ teaspoon cinnamon

CHIVE BUTTER

1 stick butter
3 heaping tablespoons
    sour cream
2 tablespoons fresh chives,
    minced

∽ Fancy Looking Butter ∾

Four pretty ways to serve butter are not as difficult as they seem. Serve the butter in a well-chilled dish, or in a special butter server that has a rack for the butter above shaved ice or icewater. Use stick butter or block butter—firm, not softened.

BUTTER BALLS 1

Cut a stick into half-inch slices. Pour boiling water over your corrugated wooden butter paddles, known as "Scotch Hands," then dip them in ice water. Place a slice of butter on one paddle and work the crisscrossed paddles as if they were the flat palms of your hands to roll a corrugated butter ball. Put balls on ice or in ice water immediately. You may be able to make a few balls before re-heating and icing the paddles.

BUTTER BALLS 2

Use a melon baller, dipped in hot water, to scoop balls out of a block.

BUTTER CURLS

Use an implement called a butter curler to scrape shell-like corrugated ovals from block butter.

DECORATED BUTTER PATS

Cut a stick into quarter-inch slices. Lightly press herb leaves into the tops. Or make paper stencils—star, heart, leaf, crescent moon—lay over butter pat and sprinkle with mild paprika or cinnamon.

"When the bread rises in the oven, the heart of the housewife rises with it."
Frederika Bremer

This is a recipe from_____   Yields:_____   Serves:_____

Ingredients:_____   _____
_____   _____
_____   _____
_____   _____
_____   _____
_____   _____
_____
_____

Directions:_____
_____
_____
_____
_____
_____
_____
_____
_____
_____

Notes:_____
_____   Date first tried:_____

This is a recipe from _____ Yields: _____ Serves: _____

Ingredients: _____

_____

_____

_____

_____

_____

_____

Directions: _____

_____

_____

_____

_____

_____

_____

_____

_____

Notes: _____

_____ Date first tried: _____

This is a recipe from _____ Yields: _____ Serves: _____

Ingredients: _____

_____ _____

_____ _____

_____ _____

_____ _____

_____ _____

_____ _____

Directions: _____

_____

_____

_____

_____

_____

_____

_____

_____

Notes: _____

_____ Date first tried: _____

Pat-a-cake, pat-a-cake, baker's man!
(So I will, master), as fast as I can:
Pat it, and prick it, and mark it with T,
Put it in the oven for Tommy and me.

Old nursery rhyme

This is a recipe from _____   Yields: _____   Serves: _____

Ingredients: _____

_____   _____

_____   _____

_____   _____

_____   _____

_____   _____

Directions: _____

_____

_____

_____

_____

_____

_____

_____

_____

Notes: _____

_____   Date first tried: _____

"Drab is the town as a shawl-hooded crone,
And dreary and cold with a chill all its own.
You ask them for bread and they give you a scone,
In Glasgow."

Arthur Guiterman

This is a recipe from _____ Yields: _____ Serves: _____

Ingredients: _____   _____

_____   _____

_____   _____

_____   _____

_____   _____

_____

Directions: _____

_____

_____

_____

_____

_____

_____

Notes: _____

_____   Date first tried: _____

This is a recipe from _____   Yields: _____   Serves: _____

Ingredients: _____

_____   _____

_____   _____

_____   _____

_____   _____

_____

_____   _____

Directions: _____

_____

_____

_____

_____

_____

_____

_____

_____

Notes: _____

_____   Date first tried: _____

97

Little Tom Tucker
Sings for his supper;
What shall he eat?
White bread and butter.
How shall he cut it,
Without e'er a knife?
How will he be married
Without e'er a wife?

Old nursery rhyme

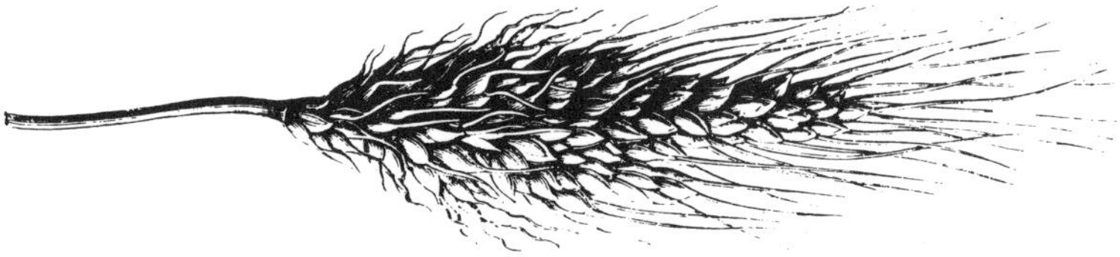

*This is a recipe from*_____ *Yields:*_____ *Serves:*_____

*Ingredients:*_____

_____

_____

_____

_____

_____

*Directions:*_____

_____

_____

_____

_____

_____

_____

*Notes:*_____

_____ *Date first tried:*_____

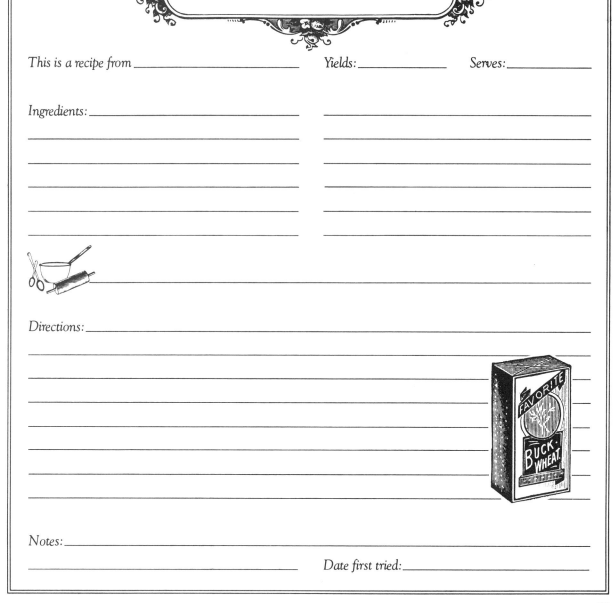

This is a recipe from _____ Yields:_____ Serves:_____

Ingredients:_____ _____
_____ _____
_____ _____
_____ _____
_____ _____
_____ _____

_____

Directions:_____
_____
_____
_____
_____
_____
_____
_____
_____

Notes:_____
_____ Date first tried:_____

This is a recipe from _____ Yields: _____ Serves: _____

Ingredients: _____ _____

_____ _____

_____ _____

_____ _____

_____ _____

_____ _____

_____

Directions: _____

_____

_____

_____

_____

_____

_____

_____

_____

_____

Notes: _____

_____ Date first tried: _____

"There is no one thing upon which health
and comfort in a family so much depend as *bread*."

Mrs. Cornelius

This is a recipe from _____ Yields:_____ Serves:_____

Ingredients:_____ _____
_____ _____
_____ _____
_____ _____
_____ _____
_____ _____
_____

Directions: _____
_____
_____
_____
_____
_____
_____
_____
_____
_____

Notes: _____
_____ Date first tried:_____

"Better is halfe a lofe than no bread."

John Heywood

This is a recipe from _____ Yields: _____ Serves: _____

Ingredients: _____ _____

_____ _____

_____ _____

_____ _____

_____ _____

_____ _____

Directions: _____

_____

_____

_____

_____

_____

_____

_____

Notes: _____

_____ Date first tried: _____

Blow, wind, blow! and go, mill, go!
That the miller may grind his corn;
That the baker may take it,
And into rolls make it,
And send us some hot in the morn.

Old nursery rhyme

This is a recipe from _____ Yields: _____ Serves: _____

Ingredients: _____

_____

_____

_____

_____

_____

_____

Directions: _____

_____

_____

_____

_____

_____

_____

_____

Notes: _____

_____ Date first tried: _____

This is a recipe from _____ Yields:_____ Serves:_____

Ingredients:_____ _____

_____ _____

_____ _____

_____ _____

_____ _____

_____ _____

_____ _____

Directions:_____

_____

_____

_____

_____

_____

_____

_____

_____

Notes:_____

_____ Date first tried:_____

"With good bread the coarsest fare is tolerable; without it, the most luxurious table is not comfortable."

Mrs. Cornelius

This is a recipe from _____ *Yields:* _____ *Serves:* _____

Ingredients: _____

_____

_____

_____

_____

_____

_____

Directions: _____

_____

_____

_____

_____

_____

_____

_____

Notes: _____

_____ *Date first tried:* _____

This is a recipe from _____ Yields: _____ Serves: _____

Ingredients: _____   _____

_____   _____

_____   _____

_____   _____

_____   _____

_____   _____

_____   _____

Directions: _____

_____

_____

_____

_____

_____

_____

_____

_____

Notes: _____

_____ Date first tried: _____

"Man can live without spices, but not without wheat."
Midrash: Psalms, 2:16

This is a recipe from _____ Yields: _____ Serves: _____

Ingredients: _____   _____

_____   _____

_____   _____

_____   _____

_____   _____

_____   _____

_____

Directions: _____

_____

_____

_____

_____

_____

_____

_____

Notes: _____

_____ Date first tried: _____

This is a recipe from _____ Yields: _____ Serves: _____

Ingredients: _____ _____

_____ _____

_____ _____

_____ _____

_____ _____

_____

_____

Directions: _____

_____

_____

_____

_____

_____

_____

_____

_____

_____

Notes: _____

_____ Date first tried: _____

1 Mamma's gone to do shopping
         And cook has a beau;
What to do with myself
         I really don't know!

2 Let me think! Oh, yes;
         I know what I'll do;
I'll bake some real bread;
         You shall see when I'm through.

3 Now, first comes the flour,
         Dumped out in a pan;
And the "rising," I think,
         Is kept in this can.

4 Oh, no! That's a powder!
         Cook says yeast is best;
I'll have some sent down
         While I'm fixing the rest.

"SEND A CAKE
OF YEAST
AT ONCE."
"YES, or COURSE,
SEND THE BEST
KIND—
FLEISCHMANN'S."

5   Now, I'll knead it up well,
           Then set it to rise;
O dolly!   Won't Mamma
          Be " awful " surprised?

6   And now into the oven
          To bake nice and brown;
'Twill be done before Mamma
         Gets back from down town.

7   We'll set my doll's table
          And all have a feast.
My !   Baking's no trouble
        If you use Fleischmann's Yeast.

8   Now, look, Dolly and Kittie,
          At the bread I have made;
I'll spread some with butter
         And peach marmalade.

This is a recipe from _____   Yields: _____   Serves: _____

Ingredients: _____   _____
_____   _____
_____   _____
_____   _____
_____   _____
_____

Directions: _____
_____
_____
_____
_____
_____
_____
_____
_____

Notes: _____
_____   Date first tried: _____

"Borsht and bread make your cheeks red."

Old Jewish proverb

This is a recipe from _____ Yields: _____ Serves: _____

Ingredients: _____ _____

_____ _____

_____ _____

_____ _____

_____ _____

_____ _____

_____

Directions: _____

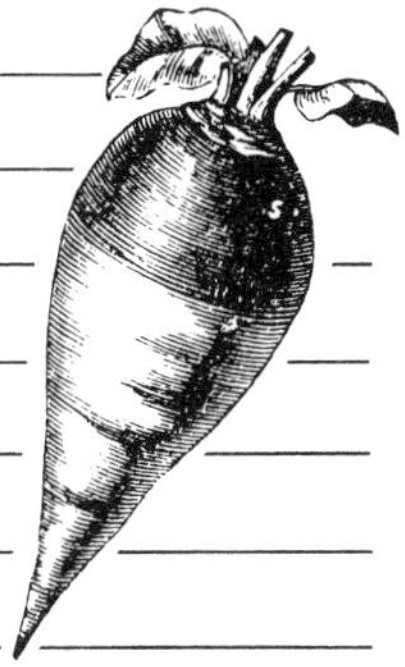

_____

_____

_____

_____

_____

_____

_____

_____

_____

Notes: _____

_____ Date first tried: _____

The lion and the unicorn
were fighting for the crown;
The lion beat the unicorn
All round about the town.
Some gave them white bread,
and some gave them brown;
Some gave them plum-cake,
And sent them out of town.

Old nursery rhyme

This is a recipe from _____ *Yields:* _____ *Serves:* _____

Ingredients: _____ _____

_____ _____

_____ _____

_____ _____

_____ _____

_____ _____

_____

Directions: _____

_____

_____

_____

_____

_____

_____

_____

_____

Notes: _____

_____ *Date first tried:* _____

This is a recipe from _____ Yields:_____ Serves:_____

Ingredients: _____

_____

_____

_____

_____

_____

Directions: _____

Notes: _____

_____ Date first tried: _____

"Bread is the staff of life."
Jonathan Swift

This is a recipe from _____ Yields: _____ Serves: _____

Ingredients: _____   _____

_____   _____

_____   _____

_____   _____

_____   _____

_____

Directions: _____

_____

_____

_____

_____

_____

_____

_____

Notes: _____

_____   Date first tried: _____

This is a recipe from _____   Yields: _____   Serves: _____

Ingredients: _____   _____

_____   _____

_____   _____

_____   _____

_____   _____

_____   _____

_____

Directions: _____

_____

_____

_____

_____

_____

_____

_____

_____

Notes: _____

_____   Date first tried: _____

The king was in his counting-house
Counting out his money;
The queen was in the parlour
Eating bread and honey; . . .

Old nursery rhyme

This is a recipe from _____ Yields:_____ Serves:_____

Ingredients:_____ _____

_____ _____

_____ _____

_____ _____

_____ _____

_____ _____

Directions:_____

_____

_____

_____

_____

_____

_____

_____

_____

Notes:_____

_____ Date first tried:_____

"Here is bread, which strengthens man's heart, and therefore called the staff of life."

Mathew Henry

This is a recipe from _____   Yields: _____   Serves: _____

Ingredients: _____   _____

_____   _____

_____   _____

_____   _____

_____   _____

_____

Directions: _____

_____

_____

_____

_____

_____

_____

_____

Notes: _____

_____   Date first tried: _____

FLOUR

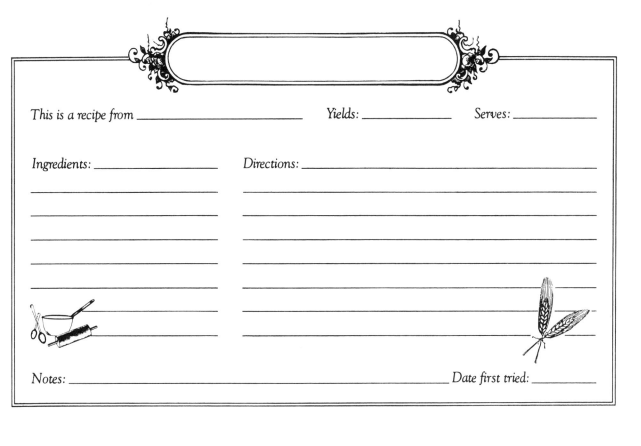

This is a recipe from _____   Yields: _____   Serves: _____

Ingredients: _____   Directions: _____

_____   _____

_____   _____

_____   _____

_____   _____

_____   _____

_____   _____

_____   _____

Notes: _____ Date first tried: _____

This is a recipe from _____   Yields: _____   Serves: _____

Ingredients: _____   Directions: _____

_____   _____

_____   _____

_____   _____

_____   _____

_____   _____

_____   _____

_____   _____

Notes: _____ Date first tried: _____

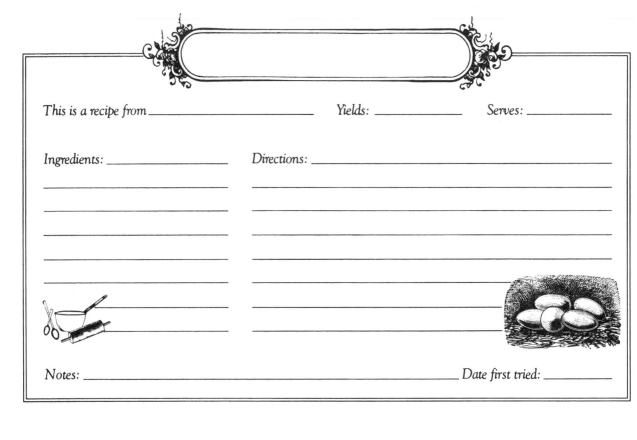

This is a recipe from _____ Yields: _____ Serves: _____

Ingredients: _____ Directions: _____

_____ _____

_____ _____

_____ _____

_____ _____

_____ _____

_____ _____

_____ _____

Notes: _____ Date first tried: _____

This is a recipe from _____ Yields: _____ Serves: _____

Ingredients: _____ Directions: _____

_____ _____

_____ _____

_____ _____

_____ _____

_____ _____

_____ _____

_____ _____

Notes: _____ Date first tried: _____

This is a recipe from _____ Yields: _____ Serves: _____

Ingredients: _____

_____

_____

_____

_____

_____

_____

Directions: _____

_____

_____

_____

_____

_____

_____

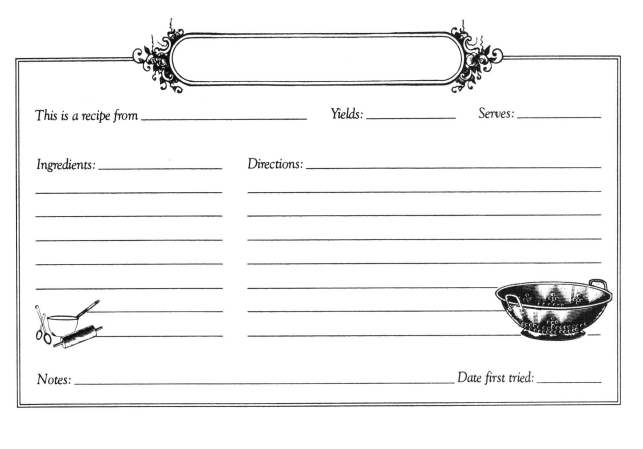

Notes: _____ Date first tried: _____

This is a recipe from _____ Yields: _____ Serves: _____

Ingredients: _____

_____

_____

_____

_____

_____

Directions: _____

_____

_____

_____

_____

_____

Notes: _____ Date first tried: _____

This is a recipe from _____ Yields: _____ Serves: _____

Ingredients: _____

Directions: _____

_____

_____

_____

_____

_____

_____

Notes: _____ Date first tried: _____

This is a recipe from _____ Yields: _____ Serves: _____

Ingredients: _____

Directions: _____

_____

_____

_____

_____

_____

_____

Notes: _____ Date first tried: _____

This is a recipe from _____ Yields: _____ Serves: _____

Ingredients: _____ Directions: _____

_____ _____

_____ _____

_____ _____

_____ _____

_____ _____

_____ _____

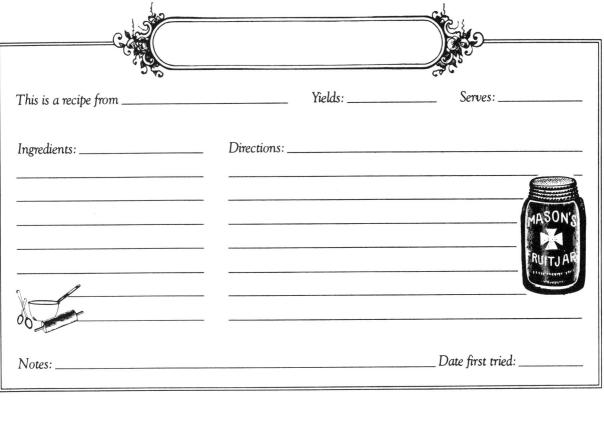

Notes: _____ Date first tried: _____

This is a recipe from _____ Yields: _____ Serves: _____

Ingredients: _____ Directions: _____

_____ _____

_____ _____

_____ _____

_____ _____

_____ _____

_____ _____

Notes: _____ Date first tried: _____

The following equipment list was culled from the recipes. Really essential are loaf pans, muffin tins, baking sheets, mixing bowls, saucepan, measuring cups and spoons, mixing spoons, rolling pin, biscuit cutter, oven thermometer, cooling racks and a timer; with that small battery of equipment, most of the recipes can be made. All dimensions and capacities are approximate —manufacturers are not consistent.

━━━ ► Equipment List ◄ ━━━

LOAF PANS: $5'' \times 2\frac{1}{2}'' \times 2\frac{1}{4}''$;
   $8'' \times 4'' \times 2\frac{1}{2}''$; $9'' \times 5'' \times 3''$

MUFFIN TINS: varying sizes

MUFFIN RINGS

BAKING DISHES: square,
   round or rectangular,
   8" square & 9" round = 6 cups

GEM PAN, and/or POPOVER PAN: cast iron

CUSTARD CUPS: 5 or 6 ounce size

TURK'S-HEAD MOLD: $1\frac{1}{2}$ or 2 quart size

TUBE PAN: 10" size

CHRISTMAS TREE CAKE PAN

CASSEROLE DISHES: $1\frac{1}{2}$ and 2 quart size

COFFEE CANS: 1 pound or

STEAMING MOLDS: 1 quart size

BAKING SHEETS: $14'' \times 16''$ or $17'' \times 26''$

KETTLE, HAM BOILER or DEEP ROASTER
   with LID: to hold 3 coffee cans

MIXING BOWLS: small, medium & large

SAUCEPANS: 1 and 2 quart size

DOUBLE BOILER: 2 quart size

SKILLET: 9" or 10" size, cast iron

FRY BASKET

MEASURING CUPS: 1, 2 & 4 cup size

MEASURING SPOONS: $\frac{1}{4}$ tsp–1 TBS

SIFTER: 4 cup capacity

FLOUR DREDGER: $1\frac{1}{2}$ cup

MIXING SPOONS: wooden & sturdy

PASTRY BLENDER

BREAD KNIFE

PARING KNIFE

DOUGH SCRAPER or SPACKLING KNIFE

GRATER: fine to coarse grids

CITRUS PEELER

GARLIC PRESS

ROLLING PIN

RUBBER SPATULA or SCRAPER

BISCUIT CUTTER

COOKIE CUTTERS: bridge set

POTATO RICER

EGGBEATER

WHISK

PASTRY BRUSH

THERMOMETERS: oven; food (0°–220°F);
   deep frying (up to 450°F)

BISCUIT BRAKE or KNEADER or,

MEAT GRINDER: hand-cranked, coarse disc

DOUGH BOARD

DISH TOWELS; PLASTIC WRAP; WAXED PAPER

COOLING RACKS

GRIDDLE SCREEN

MELON BALLER

BUTTER CURLER

BUTTER HANDS

BEETLE, MEAT POUNDER or WOODEN MALLET

MORTAR & PESTLE

CAKE TESTER

TIMER: 2 hour capability

ELECTRIC BLENDER; and ELECTRIC HAND MIXER

INDEX

Write in Your Own Index

_____
_____
_____
_____
_____
_____
_____
_____
_____
_____
_____
_____
_____
_____
_____
_____
_____
_____
_____
_____